'Marcus Osborne's long-awaited book redefines branding in Asia'

'A five-star triumph... this has to be SE Asia's business book of the year'

'Dismantles many old myths and offers fascinating observations and remedies for Asian businesses to rethink their approach to branding and communications'

'Marcus Osborne knows just how important collecting the right data is – and what to do with it when you've got it'

'A rare voice of sanity and depth in the over-hyped and shallow world of branding in Asia'

'Branding is not about logos or ad campaigns. As this book makes clear, it is the total experience of the brand, as perceived by the customer'

STOP ADVERTISING
START BRANDING

How to Build the Brand That Will Build your Business

Marcus Osborne

Matador
9 Priory Business Park,
Wistow Road, Kibworth Beauchamp,
Leicestershire. LE8 0RX
Tel: 0116 279 2299
Email: books@troubador.co.uk
Web: www.troubador.co.uk/matador
Twitter: @matadorbooks

ISBN 978 1785892 509

British Library Cataloguing in Publication Data.
A catalogue record for this book is available from the British Library.

Printed and bound by CPI Group (UK) Ltd, Croydon, CR0 4YY
Typeset in 11pt Aldine401 BT by Troubador Publishing Ltd, Leicester, UK

Matador is an imprint of Troubador Publishing Ltd

For my mother – no longer with us, but with me every day of my life

CONTENTS

Contents

Make Money, Save Money, Build Your Business

The world is changing fast. Business in Asia is changing even faster.

There are fantastic new opportunities for those who know how to use the new technologies and the new environment they've created. But there are dreadful pitfalls lying in wait for those who don't adapt or who leap into this new world without a real understanding of how to make the most of it.

This book is about branding – real, credible, profitable, customer-winning, customer-retaining branding that goes far beyond the old concepts of mass marketing.

- *It will tell you how to make money, save money and build a business that can grow from strength to strength, year after year.*
- *It will show you how to use the power of social media, improve the way you deal with customers at every touchpoint and build a 'human', likeable brand – all without the help of a massive advertising budget.*

'Stop advertising, start branding' is not just a snappy title. It's the key to business success. It's about exploiting the power of new skills and new technologies and coupling them with some old disciplines that often get forgotten.

I know this can work, right here, right now, for organisations of all shapes and sizes in Malaysia, Singapore and the other noisy, competitive and increasingly turbulent markets of Southeast Asia. My company, Fusionbrand, is working every day with private companies and public sector bodies across the region and we're seeing amazing results as our clients combine their own ideas and energy with our insider knowledge and practical skills.

If you want to know how this branding revolution can work for you, read on and you'll get the full benefit of our experience. In just a few hours, this book can change the way you run your business. And if you could do with a little help in putting these new ideas into practice, just pick up the phone.

'My job is not tweeting on my customers' behalf. It's solving problems. I use my brain and my experience to solve specific problems for specific companies in specific situations'

CHAPTER I

Take It from Me, It's All About Keeping Customers

For the last 40 years or so, it's been a cliché of the marketing world that acquiring a customer costs five times as much as retaining one. You wouldn't always guess from their behaviour that marketers and chief executives believed it, but no-one ever seems to question this piece of received wisdom.

It sounds about right, doesn't it? There's an instinctive common sense about it that makes it seem like an attractive and plausible proposition. But where did it come from? Everyone just says 'Research shows...' and moves swiftly on.

Well, I have a vested interest in this idea, as customer retention is one of the key elements in branding – and branding's my business. But I don't like taking anything like this on trust. So I thought it might be interesting to trace it back and find out when and where the cliché originated.

The first surprise was that I couldn't find any specific reference to the 5 to 1 ratio in the marketing literature of the 1960s and 1970s. There were marketing experts and academics suggesting that holding onto your customers and thinking in terms of 'lifetime value' was generally a smart way of doing business, but nothing from that era seems to identify a 5 to 1 ratio as a general rule of thumb.

It was only during the 1980s that the idea began take hold.

And it all started with an interesting but statistically flimsy research project that looked at the US automotive industry.

The original study that seems to be the source of this 5 to 1 ratio is some work on new car sales in America that was done by TARP, the pioneering customer experience consultancy, round about 1980. It was picked up and publicised over the years that followed by Harvard academics like Earl Sasser and James Heskett. When they quoted it in a *Harvard Business Review* article, it became an unassailable truth.

Then everybody's favourite business guru of the 1990s, Tom Peters, repeated it in *Thriving on Chaos* and it was soon assimilated as one of those things that everyone in business knows.

But the TARP research itself was extremely rough and ready. The sample size was small, the 'cost of acquiring a new customer' was simply the advertising spend divided by the number of new buyers and what was measured in relation to customer retention was just the 'goodwill expense' required to keep a customer. How much customer support and service was built into that figure was never stated. There are many industries and sectors that have very different dynamics from new car sales and the TARP study did not ever claim to provide any way of extrapolating the results to different territories or product types – or to business-to-business selling.

So it's important to understand that this multiple of 5 to 1 is more a figure of speech than a number you can use.

In fact, although people focused on the ratio of 5 to 1, later TARP research projects indicated that the real ratio often varied wildly, from about 20 to 1 right down to 2 to 1.

True, even a 2 to 1 ratio is something positive to work with, and a useful reminder that retention is an important source of profit. But the idea that you can do any useful sums – setting budgets, for example – by multiplying or dividing by five is not far short of nonsense.

While most companies can tell you fairly accurately how much they spend on their sales force and their marketing efforts, there are very few that can give you any kind of cash figure for their expenditure on customer retention.

This key aspect of long-term brand building demands commitment and effort from many people in many different roles across the organisation. It requires well-thought-out processes, real attention to detail and a clear intention to go the extra mile. And it cannot be switched on at will, in the way a new advertising campaign can be launched with a specific budget on a specific date.

Customer retention depends on collecting the right data about the people who buy from you, getting to know them, developing relationships that add value for them and then making the most of these relationships to build loyalty, create upselling opportunities and encourage referrals and positive customer-generated content about your products. Serving your customers well and surprising and delighting them whenever possible is the key to keeping them coming back for more.

Luckily, most companies deliver superior customer service. At least, that's what they tell researchers. Every time. When Bain & Co surveyed more than 350 firms a few years ago, 80 per cent of them said they gave their customers a 'superior experience'.

Just to be on the safe side, though, Bain then went a step further and asked the customers involved what the situation looked like from their perspective. Instead of four companies out of five delivering a 'superior experience', the customers said it was roughly one company in twelve.

Silly customers. How could they get it so wrong?

What that means, of course, is that despite the smug delusions of arrogant managers, only 8 per cent of these companies were delivering.

Bain called that yawning chasm between the 80 per cent and the 8 per cent 'the delivery gap'. The Believers took it for granted that they were right, and that what they were delivering was superior – in just the same way that 88 per cent of motorists believe they are better and safer than the average driver.

On the other hand, the 8 per cent – the one in twelve who stood out as Achievers, because they did deliver a 'superior customer experience' – were constantly listening and tweaking and working to ensure they stayed on the right side of the divide. In other words, those who had most to be proud about didn't sit around preening themselves and boasting about their performance. They left that to the people who knew better than their customers.

It's a simple, unalterable fact that the customer experience can only ever exist in the eye of the beholder. This is one area where the customer – so often wrong about so many things, though it seems blasphemous to spell out what we all know – is always right. By definition. Even a customer who actually receives lousy service but, for some reason, walks away smiling has had a good customer experience. And there's an end to it.

You've probably seen this for yourself in day-to-day situations, like those that occur in hospitals. Patients who may, objectively, have received fairly poor treatment or been made to wait for unreasonably long times may still come away feeling their overall experience has been good. One reason for this may be the unacknowledged hierarchy of elements within a typical customer experience. Some things simply matter more than others. And the bad news for those who like to systematise everything is that the most highly rated factors are those that depend most on the personal attitudes and qualities of the staff who are delivering the experience.

A few years ago, BA asked a large sample of travellers at airports around the world what they wanted most in terms of customer service and the customer experience. There was some variation, of course, but the overall shape of the results was clear and unmistakable. The customers wanted just four things.

They wanted service that was:

1. Friendly and caring
2. Flexible in its delivery
3. Capable of solving their problems
4. Able to recover from mistakes

These results caused some consternation. The problem was that BA had been working hard to improve its systems and reporting procedures and its fault-finding and error-tracking. It had invested millions in this work, and all the numbers showed that the airline's performance had steadily improved.

But the disconcerting fact was that the payoffs from all this effort were focused almost entirely on factors 3 and 4, on being able to solve problems and recover from mistakes. And, although these were clearly important, they were not at the top of the customers' list. All they wanted – or, at least, what they wanted most of all – was for all the people they came into contact with to be friendly and caring.

As an employer, there's a lot you can do. You can train people to be polite and incentivise them to be helpful and respond quickly to a request or to the sight of a customer looking lost or baffled. You can insist that telephones are answered within four rings or that no customer has to stand at a counter for more than five seconds without someone offering service or advice.

You can go right back to the recruitment stage, as some employers have done, and tell your interviewers that the company is seriously interested in recruiting the smiliest staff it can find.

The successful London-based sandwich and snacks company Prêt à Manger does just that and makes a point of wearing its smile on its sleeve. (Interestingly, Prêt sends job applicants for a one-day trial in one of its outlets and lets the staff there decide, at the end of the day, whether the potential recruit is cheery and hardworking enough.)

Google, with its lounge spaces, massage chairs and pinball machines, doesn't recruit on the basis of people's euphoria quotient, but certainly wants its staff to be as happy and positive as possible. The underlying assumption, probably well founded, is that happier people are nicer to those they have contact with.

But, of course, friendliness and caring can't actually be mandated. They can be encouraged and facilitated, but they can't be enforced. In face-to-face interactions, they are either there or they're not. You can give people all the training in the world, but you can't make them friendly and caring.

However – and this is something I will come back to in detail later on – there is a crucial difference here between face-to-face meetings and online contacts. The tone and helpfulness of a web chat conversation with a customer service agent is something that management can influence immediately and directly. And the way a company interacts with its customers and prospects across the various social media channels can go a long way towards creating and substantiating an impression of friendliness.

Like a lot of the advice I have included in this book, this is really a matter of common sense. It isn't rocket science. It's more a question of identifying the basics and doing them properly and consistently. And that applies just as much to making the most of social media as it does to the other parts of your branding journey.

The problem is, though, that there are not many real experts in the world of social media for business.

There aren't many in the US or Europe, and there are even fewer in Asia. Even the basics are often disputed, and there are a lot more people pontificating about how to build brands in today's social economy than there are doing anything significant. Everyone's a branding expert, until you ask to see what they've done to prove their worth.

I am not a theoretician or an academic, but I have gained more practical experience in these markets than almost anyone else, simply because I happened to be here, on the spot, when the social media explosion started to take place. As the world starting moving in on the SE Asian markets, I was already here in Kuala Lumpur, running a specialist branding consultancy that found itself right in the first rank of pioneers.

I started working with the new tools like Twitter and LinkedIn and Facebook at a very early stage, partly because the smaller companies that formed the bulk of my client list had limited branding budgets and needed to make every penny count. Together, we worked out new ways to combine email, direct mail and the traditional tools of the mass economy with the new tools of the internet, producing results that were often spectacular.

I had big corporate and public sector clients, too, but they could afford to spend large sums on media advertising and were slower to see the internet as anything more than another channel through which to push out their products. My business competitors were mainly advertising agencies and they were also wedded to traditional big-budget media campaigns – not least, I imagine, because big campaigns mean big commission.

So I was catapulted into the front line and had to think and learn fast. We had many early successes, including some on tiny budgets, where smart thinking had to make up for lack of spending power. I wouldn't say there were any failures, but, inevitably, there were some disappointments and some ideas

I thought would work well that didn't take off like I hoped they would. And as we banked up more and more experience, I kept looking over my shoulder to see if the competition was catching up. It hasn't happened yet. Even now, in 2016, I still haven't seen anything happening in Asia that makes me worry too much about that.

But I do think it's time someone explained to business people how we can use this combination of traditional tools and social media and laid out what we've learned so far. And since no-one else seems to be taking on that challenge, I am setting it all down in this book.

A friend of mine who runs a financial services firm looked at the outline structure I had prepared, before I sat down to start writing, and made a rather surprising comment.

'You're not going to give it all away, are you?' he asked. 'Are you mad, Marcus? If you give away all the stuff that makes you different, you won't have a business.

'You're the go-to agency for branding in the social economy, but you'll lose all your customers if you tell them how to do it themselves.'

On one level, that was an interesting reaction, because my financial friend obviously saw branding as just a matter of deploying a handful of tricks and techniques on social media. It would be like the famous secret recipe for Coca-Cola. Once people had the instructions in their hands, anyone could copy me. They'd just do it by the numbers, like assembling IKEA's flat-pack furniture. But it's really not as simple as that. The devil is in the detail, as always, and it's how you do it that makes the difference.

On another level, of course, I found my friend's attitude slightly insulting.

My job is not tweeting on my customers' behalf. It's solving problems. I use my brain and my experience to solve specific problems for specific companies in specific situations.

8

My whole career is built on the knowledge that 'one-size-fits-all' solutions rarely work and that you have to keep moving to stay ahead.

Even if I crunched down everything I'd ever learned so far and 'gave it away' in the pages of this book, I'd have moved on and developed new ideas and approaches by the time it was published, six months later. I wouldn't mind if my competitors copied my thinking all the time, as long as they promised to lag six months behind me. A six-month advantage is a big lead in this business.

So I've written my book, with nothing held back, and I am hoping it will inspire many of my readers to think afresh about branding and how it can help them grow strong and profitable businesses. In the next few hours, I will tell you all I know.

SECTION I

Put Your Money Back in Your Pocket

'Building a brand is overwhelmingly about keeping customers, rather than attracting them in the first place'

CHAPTER 2

Stop Advertising, Start Branding

I've lived in Kuala Lumpur for 21 years. My wife is Malaysian, and my children are too, in lots of ways. I've got to know the place well and I know how it works and what makes Malaysia tick. So nothing much surprises me any more. But anyone who's not familiar with the way business is done in Asia would be in for a shock if they saw the things that happen here.

I picked up my iPhone the other day and saw that a text had come in, a marketing message from a company I'd never heard of. It was short and to the point. It told me about some luxury condominium apartments that had just been built and that it felt sure I would be interested in seeing, with a view to buying one as an investment. The price was RM500,000, about US$120,000 or £75,000, and units were being offered now with a remarkable discount of 10 per cent.

But there was a kicker, too, to get my attention.

If I bought immediately, I would get a free rice cooker.

A free rice cooker? Why would a free rice cooker worth RM100 have any influence at all on my decision to spend RM500,000? What kind of marketing is that?

The answer is, it's marketing for fools. Only a fool would be influenced. And it's marketing by fools. Only a fool would waste money on such a hopelessly feeble and irrelevant promotion.

There are some – a few – very shrewd sales and marketing brains at work in Malaysia and the other countries of Southeast Asia. But there are an awful lot of people whose thinking is stuck in the Stone Age. They've got the 21st-century technology of mobiles and social media, tablets and multi-channel TV. What they haven't got is the 21st-century thinking to go with it.

To be fair, I shouldn't have called it 'Stone Age thinking'. That's not fair on the Neanderthals, who were forced by circumstance to do all their marketing face to face and may, for all we know, have made a good job of it. This kind of rice-cooker marketing is more like the 1950s, the world of *Mad Men*, the world that prompted David Ogilvy to warn his fellow ad agency manipulators: 'The consumer is not a moron; she is your wife.'

I felt annoyed, even insulted, by that crass text message the other day. But the developers were selling residential properties. Their reasoning would presumably be that they would never have any repeat buyers. Each sale would be a one-off, so they didn't need to build a brand. They were playing the numbers game – just throwing text messages out there to as many people as possible, and hoping some of it would stick. That would be their excuse for shouting their wares in the crudest possible way.

It's not like that for most of us. Most products, from cars, which many people buy every few years, to drinks and food that people buy every day, need branding. Because building a brand is the very best way of all to stay in business, stay profitable and grow bigger.

I spend my life thinking about branding, so maybe I should let you know, first of all, what it really means to me.

Building your brand is overwhelmingly about *keeping* customers, rather than attracting them in the first place.

I firmly believe that, though it's not the way most marketing people approach the world.

Just think about it. If every customer you ever had came back over and over again and never left you, it would hardly matter how slowly the numbers built up. Fast or slow, the business would grow. If every new customer became a convert for life, most of the risks would be taken out of running your business. You'd be able to plan your sales and production, predict your cashflow, know when to open and when to close, recruit the right people at the right time and know exactly when to commit yourself to a new factory or a new supply contract.

In a situation like that, the only way is up.

Unfortunately, though, it's not going to happen. Customers don't just come. They go, too. Repeat business and customer retention rates are never going to be anywhere near 100 per cent in practice. Customers will leave. But the absolute key to building a brand is getting more of them to stay.

★ ★ ★

How do you get more customers to stay? Obviously, by offering something that's more attractive to your customers than the offer your competitors are putting up against it.

Your product – and I will generally use the word 'product' here, though exactly the same arguments apply to a service as well – may perform better, look more attractive, last longer or be more readily available, when and where the buyers want to buy. It may be packaged in a form that suits customers' needs better. It may be a better fit with other items they already own. Or it may be cheaper.

These are the kind of differentiators conventional businesses around the world rely on. And which is the quickest and easiest factor to change and the one most likely to catch the customer's eye?

Price, of course.

I remember a lecture at the London Business School nearly twenty years ago where Professor Hermann Simon, Europe's leading pricing guru, tore into those who tried to buy volume by selling at impossibly low prices.

'Any fool can reduce a price with the stroke of a pen,' he said. 'And any fool can trigger the sort of price war that turns into a race to the bottom.'

Professor Simon, who went on to write *Manage for Profit, Not for Market Share*, among many other important management books, has always been a fan of companies like IKEA and Aldi that design and build themselves products or systems that give them a genuine price advantage. I am, too. But that's not the same as slashing prices by giving away your profit margin.

In Asia, there are far too many businesses that choose to make price their main differentiator. We've seen it again and again. And very few of them can survive long, if they do it by sacrificing margins.

There is always someone – in China, Bangladesh or Malaysia, or, these days, in Myanmar, Vietnam or Cambodia – who can produce the goods more cheaply. Unless you have developed some secret ingredient that will allow you to make strong profits at low prices, this kind of aggressive pricing is not a sustainable business strategy.

Some informed observers even believe that pricing is becoming less important. A recent Gartner survey reported that – within the technology sector, at least – more than 60 per cent of customers now think that customer experience may be more influential than price in buying decisions.

'By 2020,' the Gartner report said, 'customer experience will overtake price and product as the key brand differentiator.'

And it's not only your pricing that can be undermined by competitors using the cheapest overseas producers. Your other key differentiators – including performance, features and stylish design – can all be copied or improved upon by determined companies that are prepared to scour the world for new suppliers. The stark fact is that there is always someone, somewhere, who can do it better.

So how can you hope to keep your customers in a business environment where none of these traditional competitive advantages is sustainable?

The one advantage that cannot be duplicated is your company's relationship with its customers. And good relationships are the key to repeat business.

Asian companies that really want to take branding seriously, and reap the benefits, must place these customer relationships at the heart of their business planning. They must be prepared to invest in getting to know their customers by collecting the right data about them, developing relationships with them and then leveraging those relationships to generate higher sales and the referrals that will bring in more customers.

Asian businesses must understand that building brands today requires a relational, rather than transactional, approach to business.

The customer who has no relationship with you and buys solely on price will walk away and go somewhere else the moment he sees the same thing cheaper somewhere else. But customers who feel they are getting something out of the relationship, beyond the individual transaction, will stick around.

We will come back to look at this in more detail later. But that 'something' the customer gains from the relationship always depends on your ability to deliver emotional, economic and experiential value.

Of course, for a lot of segments there needs to be an emotional connection of some sort for the brand to connect with consumers before they make a purchase. But emotional value is about the depth of the relationship, the level of engagement and the degree of fit with the customer's aspirational needs. Economic value is about finding ways to ensure a greater value return to each customer than the price that was paid. Experiential value is about physical experiences with the brand, personalisation of the relationship, genuinely customer-centred processes (both at physical touchpoints and online), immediacy (in terms of how quickly needs are responded to), quality and satisfaction with the experience of interacting with the brand.

If that seems like a long and demanding shopping list, that's because it is. No-one said this was going to be easy.

But this is what needs to be done to build the relationship and nurture the brand, and it will repay every dollar and every ounce of effort. And many of these factors can be addressed now in ways that were simply not possible even five years ago. The new tools in the social media armoury can help enormously, and they are generally cheap enough for any business, large or small, to exploit. For the first time, Asian brands have the chance to compete on an almost level playing field with the global giants that have built their brands with massive advertising campaigns over many years.

Traditional ad campaigns just ate up money, for often very uncertain rewards. In the end, though, unless they completely fluffed their lines, those with the biggest budgets would almost always come out on top. Social media cannot be made to work just by throwing more money at a problem. What's needed is understanding, knowhow and a different kind of creativity.

A pilot once told me the sleek designs of modern airliners were less about aerodynamics and more about image-building than outsiders would imagine.

'With the amount of thrust today's big jet engines provide, you could pretty well make a brick fly the Pacific,' he said. 'It's all about power.'

In branding, though, brute force and ignorance won't work

any more. Mass media advertising has had its day. Building tomorrow's brands will be smarter, gentler, subtler, cheaper. But it will need new skills, new techniques, new disciplines and insights. This book will help you do it.

hard sell + ignorance won't work anymore.

SMARTER, GENTLER, SUBTLER, CHEAPER

RELATIONAL

EXPERIENTIAL, EMOTIONAL, ECONOMIC

↳ the whole   ↳ aspirations,   ↳ more value
  experience   depth of   than cost
                      relationship

'My experience shows that most companies in SE Asia could more than halve their marketing spend, if they went about it the right way — and still get better results.

Take your own money and put it back in the bank'

CHAPTER 3

Put Your Money Back in Your Pocket

There is hardly a more memorable quote in the history of marketing than Lord Leverhulme's anguished complaint: 'Half the money I spend on advertising is wasted. The problem is I don't know which half.'

At least, if you're in the UK or Europe, you'll believe it was Lord Leverhulme who uttered these immortal words. All the marketing textbooks tell you so.

It's only when you talk to Americans or read American books that you discover that everyone on that side of the Atlantic believes the same gem fell from the lips of the US retailing pioneer, John F Wanamaker. Wanamaker virtually invented advertising. He bought the world's first full-page newspaper ad in 1879 and employed the world's first-ever copywriter. The world didn't know what had hit it, and they helped make his fortune .

Wanamaker was bold, powerful and imaginative. His big idea to end the slaughter of World War I was for the US to buy Belgium from the Germans for US$100 billion, so that everyone could pack up and go home happy.

Like Leverhulme, the inventor of Sunlight Soap and founder of Lever Brothers, Wanamaker would have been well qualified to recognise the frustrations of mass market advertising. Both men profited enormously from it, but both were equally aware that much of their spending was wasted money.

I've spent several fruitless hours trying to discover which of the two business giants actually coined the famous quote, and I've come to the conclusion that no-one really knows. It seems highly likely that both will have muttered something similar at some point, but the most scrupulous histories all put '(attributed)' after the great line and nobody can point to a specific speech or piece of writing that launched it on its way in the world. So we'll probably never know.

What we do know is that, more than a hundred years later, advertisers are facing exactly the same problem. It hasn't gone away.

I've met many an advertising professional who thought 'Half my advertising is wasted, but I don't know which half' was funny. It isn't. In this day and age, it's a disgrace, an appalling indictment of the bad habits we have all got into, that we don't know, even now, whether it's half, or a third, or a quarter – or three quarters, for that matter. All we know for certain is that advertising is working even less efficiently for us now than it did 20 years ago.

There are good reasons for that. Today's better educated consumers are fed up with being lied to. Scepticism is on the increase. Media fragmentation is making it harder to launch mass advertising campaigns. And the sheer volume of audio and visual clutter makes it difficult to cut through the hubbub. The latest research shows that people are bombarded with up to 5,000 marketing messages every day, and they can only serve to cancel each other out. Our children learn to shut out the 'noise' by the time they reach their teens, just to preserve their sanity.

But the most important reason why advertising doesn't deliver value for money is even more fundamental.

Four out of five purchases are repeat purchases.

I'll repeat that, because it is one of the Great Truths of Branding. And anyone who loses sight of it is going to be in trouble.

Four times out of every five, what people buy is what they have bought before.

That's why brands work – for both consumers and business. When people find a product they like, they stay with it. That's one more decision they don't have to make when they're charging around the supermarket or hovering over the 'Buy' button online.

But if 80 per cent of transactions are repeat purchases, that means your advertising is effectively chasing after the other 20 per cent.

And if your entire advertising spend is only aimed at changing the decision in 20 per cent of people's purchases, it's not surprising that most of it is bound to be wasted.

It's time for a new approach. But most companies don't see any alternative – even now, even though they know full well the old ways aren't working. When I say 'Stop advertising, start branding', I get puzzled looks from old-school marketers, who have always behaved as if advertising, marketing and branding were the same thing.

But they're not the same. Branding is what marketing seeks to achieve. But marketing is only part of the story, and the traditional marketing toolkit is invariably centred on advertising.

It was Abraham Maslow – the same man who famously defined people's Hierarchy of Needs, from survival and safety, through love and esteem to self-actualisation – who came up with the saying 'If all you have is a hammer, everything looks like a nail.' It's become a cliché. But clichés stick around because they fit the world, and Maslow's hammer certainly sums up the traditional approach to branding.

For over a century, advertising has been the hammer – and every kind of branding problem has been the nail. When in doubt, advertisers have spent more. When that hasn't worked, they have changed agencies and tried again. And when that, too, has failed, they have upped their budgets, switched agencies again and done more of the same.

Below-the-line activity – sales promotion and pricing initiatives, PR, direct mail, point of sale, telemarketing and so on – has almost always been seen as secondary to the make-or-break impact of mass media advertising. Despite all the positive arguments about below-the-line's ability to target sub-groups and individuals, to provide tracking to prove its effectiveness and to influence purchase decisions at key moments, the lure of the big, highly visible ad campaign has usually been irresistible.

We can argue till the cows come home about whether the below-the-line tools available to previous generations were powerful enough to build major brands without mass media ad campaigns, and whether budgets should have been allocated differently.

But the advent of the internet and social media has settled the argument once and for all. It may still be possible to use big-budget ad campaigns to launch or sustain a brand, but it is now clear, beyond all doubt, that this is not the best and most cost-effective way.

And for regional companies in SE Asia that cannot hope to match the spending muscle of the global multinationals, a clever, integrated, holistic branding approach that makes full use of the power of the internet and social media is by far the best bet.

In fact, my experience shows that most companies in SE Asia could probably *halve* their marketing spend, if they went about it the right way, and still get better results.

Suppose you have a marketing budget of US$1 million.

You may decide to invest US$50,000 in employing a senior online community manager and another US$50,000 for two or three more junior support staff to help build and maintain your social media presence. You will need to set aside some money – perhaps as much as US$100,000 – for a thorough brand audit (the 'brand healthcheck'), which will take the temperature of the brand, tell you exactly where you stand with customers and provide you with the vital indications of what needs to be improved in terms of customer touchpoints, systems and processes, staff training and brand messaging. That's US$200,000 so far.

Once you have gathered this crucial information, you will have a clear picture of what you need to do to build the brand and meet your branding objectives. This can then be achieved through careful, methodical implementation, based on combining social media engagement with the use of readily available customer relationship tools, direct mail initiatives, some PR work and a certain amount of smart, highly-targeted tactical advertising. Let's allow, say, US$300,000 for these activities.

Put all the elements together and you're spending a total of US$500,000.

And the rest of your US$1 million budget?

The best place for that is right back in your bank account, where it can be made available to finance the growth and development of your business.

Take your own money and put it back in the bank. You'll be half a million dollars better off, right from the start.

The point is that what you spend on mass advertising is prayer money, an offering to the gods. Your costs are fixed, and the returns are variable. Sometimes your prayers will be answered. Usually they won't be, and you'll be left wondering how so much advertising firepower can deliver so little positive impact on sales.

I was reminded of this when I saw a full page ad the other day in Malaysia's *New Straits Times* for one of those astronomically expensive wristwatch brands – Patek Philippe, I think. It's a great product, for those with money to burn. But what the hell were they doing advertising in the *New Straits Times*? That ad will not sell them a single watch, except perhaps by coincidence.

Only a tiny percentage of that newspaper's 100,000 readers will be in the market for luxury watches – and most of them will already have decided what watch they want. A Patek Philippe may be highly desirable, but if a wealthy individual already has his heart set on a Rolex Daytona, a Vacheron Tourbillon, a Breitling or a TAG Heuer, a newspaper ad is not going to change his mind. Patek Philippe might just as well have poured its money down the drain.

So why do companies that should know better behave in such irrational ways?

In this case, the answer is almost certainly that someone back home in Switzerland came up with a top-down global advertising plan and budget for Patek Philippe.

Most of the money will have been allocated to Europe, the Middle East and North America, but a certain amount will have been earmarked for Asia. Within that Asian budget, the obvious priorities – China, India, Hong Kong and Singapore, the markets with huge populations or the richest consumers – will have been given the lion's share. But down near the bottom of the list, there will have been a certain amount set aside for advertising in countries like Malaysia, Indonesia, Vietnam and Cambodia.

Patek Philippe's people in Kuala Lumpur will probably have been handed a budget and told to do what they can with it. And because they simply don't know what else to do, the money will have ended up being spent, uselessly, on the vanity advertising I saw in the *New Straits Times*.

You don't see such obvious instances of 100 per cent wasted advertising every day. But you do see cases, every day of the week, of hopeful advertisers hurling their money into battles they can't win.

For example, food manufacturers in SE Asia ought to know by now that they can't slug it out toe-to-toe with the big global brands. Whatever you are prepared to spend, Nestlé can outspend you any time it wants to. So can Unilever, Ajinomoto, Pepsico, Heinz and a dozen others. If you pick a head-on fight with any of these giant competitors, you will first be ignored, until you become a nuisance, and then crushed underfoot, when it suits them.

The only way to grow and survive in markets dominated by this kind of competition is to develop a really tough, distinctive, durable brand that customers actively prefer and feel loyal to.

The bad news is that that's not easy. But the good news is that doing it does not have to depend on having a huge advertising budget.

By making the most of the relationship-building potential of new tools such as social media, you can make sure that none of your money is wasted. And just getting full value from your budget effectively doubles your spending power, compared with those still suffering from the curse of Lord Leverhulme and John Wanamaker and wasting half their money.

There was a wonderful example of how social media and conventional ad campaigns stack up against each other in the music business in late 2013, when both Beyoncé and Lady Gaga released their new albums. Lady Gaga's *Artpop* was backed up by a reported US$25 million advertising campaign, but it still only sold 260,000 copies in its first week. Mrs Jay-Z's people spent a tiny fraction of that, yet her *Beyoncé* album sold over a million in the first six days, simply because she was able to mobilise a massive and committed audience on Facebook.

Both Beyoncé and Gaga had more than 60 million Facebook likes. The difference was that Beyoncé's team spent weeks concentrating all its efforts on making the most of that huge asset, while the Gaga promotion machine focused on the ad campaign and failed to put in the work needed to get the momentum going on social media.

On a less dramatic level, I had an interesting experience last year of how brands can be built and extended without mass media advertising. The women in my family have always, since my mother's day, been fans of Boden, the British clothing retailer. So I looked online and bought about £100-worth of Boden bits and pieces – pyjamas, T-shirts and so on – for my girls for Christmas, arranging for delivery in the UK to my daughter, who was flying home to Kuala Lumpur a week or so later.

But something went wrong. The delivery didn't arrive, she had to get on her plane and the Christmas presents weren't going to be with us in time. After all, Boden hasn't ever claimed to deliver in SE Asia.

But it's a company that makes customer service part of its brand values. When I got in touch, the people at Boden immediately apologised and said 'Very sorry about that. We'll send it all to you straight away in Malaysia.'

They were as good as their word and the presents duly arrived in Kuala Lumpur just in time for Christmas. I liked that, and I'm hooked. Suddenly, for me, Boden has defined itself as a company that's human. It makes mistakes, but it puts them right. Most of all, it treats me like a real person, like a friend. Like I'm important. With that one quick, generous gesture, Boden got me completely on its side.

Since then, I've been getting emails from Boden. More than I'd ideally like, actually. They send them to me regularly, maybe twice a week, which is more than I really want to hear from them. I delete them. But I always open them first.

I read the Boden emails every time because they are so good – animated, fresh, interesting, topical and always relevant, with the little extra kicker of offers of 10% off here and 20% off there. Or countdown offers, where you have just 13 hours to get 30% off an award-winning cocktail dress or some other out-of-the-ordinary item.

My inbox is drowning in junk mail. I spend ten minutes every morning just deleting the junk that's streamed in overnight. But I always read the Boden emails before I get rid of them.

And I'm buying more. I'm a repeat customer now. My wife and daughter both had birthdays in May, and as I was going to be in the UK for a few days before that, I ordered £150-worth of Boden stuff for them, so that I could pick it up in London.

If you think about it, that's free revenue for Boden. There's no marketing cost. I live outside the company's delivery area, by a few thousand miles, so I'm effectively going to collect the stuff myself. There has been, obviously, no Boden advertising spend in Malaysia. The incremental cost of adding me to its mailing list of 2 million customers (55 per cent of them outside the UK) and sending me those emails is so small it's not worth even thinking about. That £150 is coming to Boden for nothing, just because of the good response to my earlier problem and the stream of interesting emails I've received since then. Boden has built a relationship with me. It's made me a fan, as well as a customer, and now I'm sharing my experiences with the readers of this book, at least some of whom will visit the company's website. And Boden is likely to be selling to me time and time again now for the next ten or twenty years, again without having to advertise.

Compare that with the typical retailer here in Kuala Lumpur, or Singapore or Jakarta, who sells me £100-worth of goods. I go in, I buy and I walk out. And that's the end of it.

I know it's harder for a store-based retailer to collect

relevant data than it is for Boden and its online peers. But there's no attempt to get any information from me or about me. The store doesn't know who I am, so it has no way to build any kind of relationship with me. The purchase is just a one-off transaction, driven by my whim or my need at the time and probably clinched by the offer of a low price. Next time I have the same whim or need, there may be a chance I'll go to the same store again, to have a look. But if a rival retailer down the road is offering even a slightly better price, that's where I will buy. I have no affection, no relationship, no loyalty, no reason to go back, rather than try somewhere else.

And because these local retailers know nothing about me and can't target me or talk to me, they can only ever hope to reach me again via costly scattergun advertising.

Boden is 6,500 miles away, yet it can talk to me any time it wants to, for the cost of an automated email. My local department store is only a couple of miles up the road, but it can't get through to me except by paying out for hit-or-miss television commercials, press ads or billboard campaigns. If I happen to go and make a coffee while the commercials are on, turn two pages at once when I'm reading the paper or glance the other way as I drive past a billboard, that money is wasted.

Businesses tend to be conservative, and Asian businesses are sometimes particularly slow off the mark. But Asia's consumers are often a lot quicker to latch on to new technologies and new lifestyles. The astonishing rate of adoption of smartphones across the whole of SE Asia has created the opportunity to build brands and customer relationships in direct and affordable ways that were simply unavailable even five years ago. Social media, text messaging and targeted communications like Boden's emails are changing the landscape. And the one thing all the new media have in common is that they don't call for anything like the spending that's needed to create and implement those old-fashioned ad campaigns.

I've never heard anyone who is using the new tools complain that half the budget is wasted. It just doesn't happen. The twin virtues of targeting and tracking mean that even if an initiative is underperforming, it is always possible to examine the data and see exactly what is going wrong.

— I see it wasted

If they were alive today, both Leverhulme and Wanamaker would undoubtedly be pioneers in making the most of the newest and most powerful tools, just as they did in their heyday. But I guarantee you wouldn't hear either of them complaining that half their advertising was wasted – or that they didn't know which half.

Can spend less.
Focus on relationship.
A company that is human

— generous response.

Distinctive audience, know them or advertising ∴ selling relationship or something looking to actually develop, be.

Whether tracking.

'It's the consumer's total experience of the brand that defines it and ultimately determines its success. That is a chain where everything depends on the weakest link. One gap, one weakness, anywhere along the line, can ruin everything'

CHAPTER 4

Why Advertising Fails –
And Branding Doesn't

I have a friend who likes cars. I'm not going to give his name, as it's not important here. But all his friends will recognise him immediately from this little story.

This man doesn't just like cars, though. He likes small luxury cars. And he likes buying them. Little and often. He's bought three in the last two years. And he likes telling people about them on his blog and Facebook page once he's bought them. If I were a luxury car maker, he's the kind of wealthy, enthusiastic buyer I would have dreams about. If I owned a dealership, I would do almost anything to get him and keep him as a regular customer and to leverage his Facebook friends and blog readers and his relationships with others to get more customers.

A couple of years ago, my friend noticed that some of the best-looking cars on the streets of KL were Audis. The coolest businessmen and the smartest women around town seemed to have switched their allegiances and taken up with Audi. Suddenly, every Mercedes he saw looked a trifle lumpy. The BMW designs struck him as pushy, rather than assertive. The Lexus models were just a bit ordinary.

He wanted an Audi. And because he doesn't have to stop and wait and plan or save for these things, he decided to get one. Nothing flashy. Just an A4. Something to use to zip around town, maybe go for drive at the weekend, down to Malacca, and get away from the city, or to let his daughter drive when she's home from her Aussie university.

When he found himself stuck at a traffic light at 5.20 one afternoon, just across from a massive electronic billboard showing a beautiful Audi A4, it almost seemed like a sign from above. He punched in the number on the ad and listened to the phone ring.

No answer. No answering machine, either.

'Not great,' he thought. 'I'll give them a call tomorrow.'

He watched as a white A4 slid past in the outside lane.

He grinned and muttered to himself.

'Yeah. That'll do nicely.'

The next day was meeting after meeting. He went online briefly to find out where the Audi showroom was. But it was a couple of days before he was able to get along there in person.

The showroom looked good. It smelt good, with that indefinable waft of luxury. And the staff looked smart. They didn't exactly rush to help him, but he approached the nearest saleswoman and explained what he wanted.

'Ah, we don't have the car you want, the A4, in stock,' she explained. 'You will have to wait three months. It costs RM240,000 and we do not give discount.'

There was something infuriatingly smug and uncaring about this woman and the way she spoke. It seemed a pity my friend had disturbed her morning. He thought of asking about fixing up a test drive, but the whole idea suddenly seemed less attractive. Perhaps the Audi wasn't so special, really. Sort of a jumped-up VW, in fact. Not a thoroughbred, built from the ground up to satisfy the discerning driver. Not like, say, the effortless quality of a Mercedes.

He left the showroom and bought his Mercedes C250 Avantgarde the following weekend.

There are some important business lessons here. One is that this man did not need a new car at all. He was only stimulated to buy at that time by his sudden feeling that he would like to have an Audi, based on the new models he saw driving around town. And Audi, through its marketing efforts – its TV commercials, billboards and newspaper and online campaigns – had initially persuaded him to buy into the idea of the brand. Yet the obvious failure to get the staffing and systems right to make the brand come alive at the crucial customer touchpoint had handed this business to a major competitor.

My friend went on to buy another two cars in the next 15 months, making three in two years. None of them was an Audi.

He still he has a hankering to own an Audi, he confessed to me, but instead he's bought a BMW and another small Mercedes. What's more, he's talked about all this several times on his Facebook page and, because it's an amusing story, partly at his own expense, he keeps telling everyone what happened. At least one other friend of his has been put off buying an Audi because of his experience.

'I wouldn't take the risk,' the friend of a friend says.

'If they're like that when you're standing there in the showroom with a bundle of cash and an immediate urge to buy, what on earth are they going to be like if something goes wrong and you need a repair under warranty?'

That's powerful negative word of mouth, with enough of a human interest angle to go modestly viral – either online or simply in terms of people passing the story on in casual conversation. The snooty woman in the showroom will end up costing Audi a lot more than the one customer.

In fact, even the Mercedes and BMW dealers from whom my friend did eventually buy his new cars didn't impress him much. He felt they only wanted to clinch the deal and sell a car. At one dealership, he was even ushered into a sales office tactlessly labelled 'Closing Room'.

None of these dealers seemed to see much benefit in getting to know him, finding out if he was important and exploring whether he really wanted an A4 or could be up- or cross-sold. They clearly didn't see the potential for building a long-term relationship that might eventually sell him not one car but two, three, four or five over the next few years. And he wasn't particularly impressed with the level of service he received, either. So it wasn't even that these rival dealerships were good. It was just that Audi had managed to create a negative impression – and it never got a second chance.

That's a key point. Because, in today's marketplace, you only get one chance to get it right. Blow that opportunity and you are playing catch-up, possibly for years to come.

It's not just the auto industry that needs to sharpen up its act. Today's brand narratives are being built in new ways. It's no longer just about corporate messaging that uses slick and beautifully executed CGI-enhanced commercials, with budgets that would make a Hollywood producer drool. Instead, it's all about getting the vital details right, from the customer's very first contact with the person representing the brand right through to the use of social media to maintain a warm and positive relationship.

It's not uncommon to see Asian firms in many different industries make the same mistakes the car companies make. I know all too many business leaders who are happy to put a fortune behind an advertising campaign but will not invest the much smaller amounts needed to get the organisational processes and systems that affect the brand right.

Millions are spent on advertising, yet the key relationship touchpoints where the brand's foundations are laid are often neglected. It's as if companies don't want to build a bond with the consumer, but prefer to rely on advertising to try to force the sales of their cars or investments or properties. They seem to be missing the point that building a brand is not about selling a product once. It is about selling it to the same customer over and over again and engaging that customer as a brand ambassador and influencer.

★ ★ ★

What lessons can we learn from my friend's Audi story? Traditionalists might say this was a perfect example of effective marketing, because it achieved its initial aim of driving the consumer towards Audi. They'd argue that the marketing was effective, but the sales execution was abysmal.

That's the wrong way to look at it.

It was bad branding, because it was incomplete branding. The point is that branding is not just about marketing or advertising or sales or PR or any other discipline in isolation. It's the consumer's total experience of the brand that defines it and ultimately determines its success. And that really is a chain where everything depends on the weakest link.

My luxury car-buying friend may have been lured in by the fortune Audi had spent on traditional mass communications – its print ads and billboards, its TV commercials and online advertising campaigns and its PR and product placement. But all that good work was undone by its poor performance at the key branding touchpoints – sales, customer engagement and service.

Audi had got him where it wanted him, in the showroom, primed and ready to buy. The test drive he never took would have been just a formality. He was as close as you can get without signing the deal.

But then it all turned to dust. In just a few moments, the bad impression created by that sales person ensured that every cent that had been spent on trying to make him buy into the brand was wasted money.

The saleswoman may not even have been all that incompetent. She may have been having a bad day or soldiering on through a headache. She may usually be lively, attentive, polite and positive. Factors like that can't always be planned for. But she was probably doing what she had been trained to do, and her training had clearly been grossly inadequate for the job of selling luxury cars to upmarket buyers. A properly trained sales person would have pounced on the opportunity to acquire a new customer and clinch an advance order for an A4, or even to upsell the buyer to an A6 or some other car that was currently in stock.

In a matter of seconds, this dealership had lost the chance to acquire a new customer, sell a car, prepare the ground for future sales and recruit a potential brand advocate. So who was to blame?

The fatal flaw in the branding may have been down to an ineffective sales manager or a second-rate training scheme. Or maybe it was just that my friend's expectations had been revved up too high by the barrage of advertising promises – and crushed by the brand's failure to deliver against those promises.

The point is that branding must be viewed holistically. One gap, one weakness, anywhere along the line, can ruin everything. In the course of this book, I will show you how to avoid making this kind of mistake, based on the latest theory and practice from the US and Europe, combined with more than twenty years' experience of the special characteristics of our Asian markets.

how committed are you to delivering
value? To making friends? To
establishing a reputation? In the
tough times this will help. B'ly
companies force sales + neglect processes.

What is the weakest link in your
brand touchpoints?

'The problem was that the Malaysia Airlines advertisements were not trying to change perceptions. They were trying to change reality. And ads can't do that'

branding is about customers total
experience of the brand.

promise + deliver

CHAPTER 5

Malaysia Airlines:
Discounting Is Not Rebuilding

In the third quarter of 2014, Malaysia Airlines went for broke, in a desperate attempt to stop its passenger numbers and yields going through the floor. The airline's hamfisted attempts to attract new customers, at almost any price, were summed up in some of the least enticing tactical advertising campaigns I have ever seen.

'You lift us up – Great fares for you' the ads mumbled.

'The experience getting there is half the fun' said another oddly-phrased campaign that appeared on Facebook pages.

If the first example failed to thrill, with its crude appeal to opportunistic bargain-hunters, who had already noticed that MAS tickets were suddenly available at fire-sale prices, the second showed a staggering lack of sensitivity to customers' perceptions.

At a moment in aviation history when the news media were full of grim images of flag-draped coffins being flown back from the Ukraine, only the MAS marketing team could possibly have imagined that it was a good idea to try to convince people that they should fly Malaysia Airlines because it would be fun.

I tackled this sensitive, controversial issue at the time, in my *brandconsultantasia.wordpress.com* blog, with a post that stirred up a lot of impassioned reactions, both for and against.

'Are they mad?' I wrote. 'Should they be trying to do that? Do they think they can change global perceptions of MAS with one grammatically incorrect tagline?'

But the problem was, of course, that the Malaysia Airlines advertisements were not trying to change perceptions. They were trying to change reality. And ads can't do that.

Malaysia Airlines was in a terrible situation, and I had and have every sympathy for the airline and its staff. As everyone knows, 2014 was a nightmare for MAS. In the space of 131 days, from 8 March to 17 July, two of its Boeing 777 aircraft were lost, with a total of 537 passengers and crew. The airline, which, despite all its business problems, had had one of the best safety records in the industry, was brought to its knees. In August, it was announced that it was to be renationalised, delisted, slimmed down, reorganised and set on a path that would hopefully bring it back into profit by late 2017.

The nightmare had begun with the disappearance of Flight MH370, lost without trace in an unknown location. This was a unique and puzzling tragedy. Even a year or more afterwards, rumours and conspiracy theories swirled around it and people still didn't know whether or not it was related to security or other failings on the airline's part.

The loss of MH17, shot down over the disputed territory of eastern Ukraine, was simply a cruel and random accident. According to flight radar records, more than 60 airlines were still using that route and flying regularly over the same area at that time. The plane that was targeted by the fatal missile could equally well have been a flight operated by Lufthansa, Emirates or Singapore Airlines. It was just Malaysia Airlines' bad luck that it was in the wrong place at the wrong time.

In the context of these terrible human tragedies, it may seem harsh to analyse the failings of the airline's marketing, then and over the previous few years. But one inescapable fact stands out.

MAS had relied very heavily on mass media advertising campaigns to keep the customers coming in. In the three years before the loss of MH370, the airline had spent more than RM1 billion (US$300 million) on advertising and promotions.

When the disasters occurred, this huge investment was nullified overnight. It was wiped from the slate, as if it had never happened. MAS had made the crucial error of mistaking advertising for branding, and it had failed to build and nurture the kind of engaged and loyal customer community that might have helped see it through the crisis.

The billion ringgit that had been spent provided no defence against the dramatic loss of confidence that hit the airline. Customers turned their backs, many flight crew left the company and the share price plummeted, despite the fact that Malaysia Airlines could well have been blameless in relation to both tragedies.

Poor handling of PR and communications after the two disasters accentuated the problems and led to considerable public hostility towards MAS. But there is no doubt that the airline could have coped with this unenviable situation much better if it had paid attention, over the previous few years, to the patient, detailed, low-key work that's needed to build a real, robust and durable brand. Instead of throwing millions at its advertising agencies and expecting them to solve its image and customer service problems, Malaysia Airlines could have built a brand that would have been a major asset in its time of need. It failed to do so, and it paid the price.

In the aftermath of the terrible loss of MH370 and MH17, MAS faced the unenviable task of trying to claw itself back from the brink. It needed to come up with a strategy to rebuild its shattered brand, at a time when even the mention of the airline's name was bound to evoke a mass of negative images. It needed a nimble, surefooted approach that would help it pull itself round from a desperate position. But many of its responses, throughout the latter half of 2014, were clumsy and ill-judged.

The foundation stone for the rebuilding process could – and should – have been the information Malaysia Airlines already had about its existing customers.

The airline's Enrich frequent flyer programme database is big and long-established, and it could have been a goldmine, offering a mass of detailed data about one million regular and loyal MAS customers, covering personal details, destinations, flying habits and preferences. It wasn't the world's greatest, in terms of data quality, but it was still a key resource. The database should have been cleaned, de-duped and leveraged to make sure that every one of these regular customers was contacted regularly and encouraged to think positively about the airline.

The focus should have been on building on these existing relationships and offering added value to these frequent travellers – and it wouldn't have taken a genius to come up with a range of suitable initiatives to keep them interested. Enrich members could have been given double miles, free stop-offs in Kuala Lumpur, hotel rooms, airport transfers and vouchers for big discounts in duty free shops. Any or all of these could have been put in place quickly and easily, at far less cost than the revenue that was forfeited by going for the panic option of offering bargain-basement fares.

There was a golden opportunity here to begin rebuilding the brand from the bottom up. But that was spurned in favour of a knee-jerk reaction that focused entirely on getting bums on seats, whatever the cost. Ticket prices were slashed, offering spectacular bargains to those who were in a position to take advantage of them. Long-haul passengers looking to book flights to the UK or Australia over the Christmas period found they could buy three tickets on MAS for the price of one seat on a top-tier competitor.

Cutting ticket prices to fire-sale levels is no way to rebuild an airline's reputation. And even the execution of this short-term tactical response was badly flawed. The ads that announced the new fare offers looked as if they had been slapped together by the office junior, with no imagery or style to speak of and the dullest possible copy lines. 'You lift us up – Great fares for you' was never going to be the most inspiring slogan and, of course, it focused entirely on price. Anyone who was likely to be attracted by that kind of offer was equally likely to be lured away the moment a competitor came up with something comparable.

You can persuade opportunists to buy almost anything once, if you drop your prices low enough. But how many of them will stick around when your pricing starts to edge up again towards sustainably profitable levels?

This dismal assumption that revenues could only be rebuilt by giving money away extended to Malaysia Airlines' dealings with travel agents as well.

Australian travel agents were offered expensive Rolex wristwatches and free trips to Europe and Asia as incentives, if they could sell a minimum of A$20,000-worth of MAS tickets. At home and abroad, agents were offered 11 per cent commission, twice the normal level, in a desperate attempt to kickstart the business. When this inflated commission was withdrawn, however, most travel agents, naturally enough, went straight back to doing exactly what they had been doing before the short-term incentive was put in place.

The fire-sale tactics simply didn't work. Yields and passenger numbers hit rock bottom and the airline was forced to delay reporting its Q3 financial results because it didn't have the details it needed.

MAS had simply failed to capitalise on one of its few remaining branding assets – the history and goodwill it had built up with its regular customers.

Frequent flyers who kept on choosing MAS, even after the twin disasters, should have been identified and given the very best treatment the airline could provide. These people should have been receiving regular, personalised communications thanking them for their support and offering them special privileges – free air miles, upgrades or other demonstrations of gratitude and appreciation – in explicit recognition of the fact that they were keeping the airline flying.

Instead, even travellers who flew 30 or more times with MAS in the months following the tragedies enjoyed no special treatment. The only emails they received from the airline were the usual ill-targeted and usually generic marketing messages that had marked MAS's previous poor performance in the area of customer relationship management.

Up to eight emails a month were streaming into frequent flyers' inboxes. But they weren't tackling the urgent task of cementing the relationship with MAS. Many of them were simply sales pitches from commercial partners such as the Mines Resort and Golf Course, south of Kuala Lumpur, and the Lewré shoe company. The database, potentially such a great asset, was obviously being made available to third parties and had clearly not been segmented in any intelligent way. Promotions for golf courses were sent out as email broadsides, with no apparent effort to target those with a particular interest in golf.

Even Malaysia Airlines' own promotions showed a sad inability to make use of the information that was already available in the database. For example, Enrich managed to come up with a scheme offering extra air miles for frequent flyer programme members who booked to stay at particular hotels. But this was sent out so indiscriminately that my 14-year-old son was invited to take advantage of the offer. How many 14-year-olds book hotel rooms? Luckily, my boy was used to such nonsense – as he reminded me, he'd been invited to apply for an MAS co-branded credit card when he was just 12.

All customers, and air travellers are no exception, are interested in just one thing: WIIFM, or what's in it for me? Those of us who had flown MAS for many years and particularly appreciated its services on some of its less glamorous routes felt we did have an interest in its continuing existence – and even its future success. We cared about the airline. But we had the same concerns about safety as everyone else, and we were not going to risk our lives or the lives of our families. At this point, we should have been given reassurance, insider information, news of engineering and security updates – anything and everything that would make us feel secure, safe and valued.

No effort should have been spared to ensure that each customer who chose MAS in these difficult times was made to feel special. And while attentive, personalised customer care should arguably have been part of the brand strategy all along, it was obvious that it had become even more important than usual under these special circumstances.

MAS had the opportunity to take these saviours of the brand and nurture the relationship to turn them into brand ambassadors, as a counterweight to the negativity engulfing the airline. At a time when the carrier's name was on everyone's lips, albeit for all the wrong reasons, the value of having loyal brand advocates who would talk long and loud about the fact that they were still flying MAS was potentially incalculable. Their influence could have done more to rebuild trust quickly than any amount of discounting or corporate advertising.

Part of the problem, though, was that Malaysia Airlines had never been very professional about asking the right questions and getting the right information from its customers. Its standard post-flight follow-up questionnaire, which was still being sent out, unaltered, to passengers in the period after the

MH370 and MH17 disasters, contained a typically routine and useless series of questions. I couldn't help noticing one glaring example of this.

'Please rate the following,' it asked. 'Value for money: Excellent, Good, Fair, Poor, or Very Poor?'

Under more ordinary circumstances, this question might have been reasonably helpful. But in the new situation, where one passenger might have paid RM50 for a deeply-discounted ticket while the person in the next seat could have been charged RM400 for the same flight, the information it yielded was always going to be suspect. Customers who had paid the full price and discovered that they had paid eight times as much as their neighbours were never likely to give a positive answer to the value-for-money question. Without knowing how much had been paid, no-one could begin to interpret the answer in any sane way.

This inability to think things through and ask questions that will gather useful and relevant data is a major weakness when it comes to personalising communications, generating offers and building the brand. As the airline market fragments into smaller and more specialised segments, an airline like MAS should be focusing on identifying and addressing these segments in very precise ways. Every potentially profitable niche will have its own needs and preferences. It is one thing to know that 20 per cent of the market for leisure travel from Japan is made up of over-65s. But it is quite another to collect enough data about this segment to be able to shape a suitable range of offerings and communicate them to potential customers through the media they favour.

This kind of activity takes insight and brainpower, as well as technique. Malaysia Airlines is not the only carrier that regularly falls short of what is required. But the aftermath of the MH370 and MH17 tragedies showed up, in horribly stark detail, the lack of branding skills that had left MAS so vulnerable and so pitifully ill-equipped to ride out the storm.

In the wake of the disasters, some of the actions that were taken at Malaysia Airlines were the right responses. There is no doubt, for example, that the decision to cut the workforce by 6,000 was something that should have been tackled much earlier. I was not the only one who had been pointing out for years that the carrier's closest rival, Singapore Airlines, had a comparable fleet (around 100 planes) and a similar route network (about 150 destinations), but managed to get by with 12,000 staff, compared with 20,000 at MAS – and incidentally made profits of about US$250m a year, while MAS lost the same amount. Every time I passed through KL International Airport, I had seen for myself how many Malaysia Airlines people seemed to be standing around, listless and underemployed, and had wondered if the carrier's management would ever have the guts to bite the bullet and cut the payroll. If nothing else, the shock to the system clearly brought it home that the workforce needed to be rationalised.

But other, equally important, changes had still not been tackled more than a year after the second plane was lost. At the time of writing, MAS had still not taken action to fix the grotesquely clunky and unhelpful booking engine on its website. It had not, apparently, realised that rebuilding an attractive and credible MAS brand would mean it needed to retrain and remotivate its cabin crews, check-in staff, baggage handlers and customer service representatives to make them the living embodiment of the brand.

There seemed to be little understanding of the way a good customer experience feeds through into loyalty and repeat business. And there was certainly no sign of the investment that was required to bring the airline's in-flight entertainment, comfort and service, its customer communications and its helplines up to the highest modern standards.

There are apparently plans afoot to update the Malaysia

Airlines uniforms, which have been largely unchanged for three decades. But the problem is not cabin crew uniforms that date back to the 1980s. The problem is a set of attitudes and marketing strategies that are just as outdated, just as firmly stuck in the Reagan/Thatcher/Lee Kuan Yew era. The carrier may or may not have contributed to the circumstances that led to two terrible disasters in quick succession. But until MAS realises that its survival will depend on building a solid, robust customer-centred brand – and that this must be lived to the full and made evident at every single touchpoint – it is doomed to struggle for years to come.

SECTION 2

Real Customers,
Real Conversations

'Nobody knows what new products, technologies and competitors are waiting round the corner. Prediction is useless, but preparation is all.

A strong brand prepares you for the unknown'

CHAPTER 6

If It's Good Enough for Kasparov…

You probably know the story of the invention of chess. The game was created in India, around 1,500 years ago. According to legend, the King was so delighted that he wanted to pay the inventor a lot of money to reward him. But the Man Who Invented Chess was already one move ahead of him.

'No, Your Majesty,' he said. 'I have no wish for money. Just give me a grain of rice on the first square of my chessboard. Then give me two grains on the second square, four on the third, eight on the fourth and so on, right up to the last square on the board.'

'Righty-ho,' said the King. 'Suit yourself. I'll get my treasurer to do the sums and arrange it for you.'

Well, you don't need me to tell you what happened next. If you've not come across this legend before, you can work it out for yourself. Or you can just take it from me that the total amount of rice involved is pretty huge. It's actually 18 million million million grains of rice ($2^{64}-1$). That would be getting on for 500,000 million tons – roughly a thousand times today's total global production of rice.

Yes, you might have known that the Man Who Invented Chess would have been no dummy.

In one version of the story, the King abdicates and the Man Who Invented Chess becomes the new king.

In another – more plausible – version, the King orders his guards to chop off the Man Who Invented Chess's head. Which just goes to show that a talent for mathematics without an understanding of human psychology can be a double-edged sword. Nobody loves a smart-arse.

When I pointed out earlier that a firm that never lost a customer would be destined to succeed, almost irrespective of how slowly it acquired new business, I suppose I had that story in the back of my mind.

What if you never lost a customer and you could get each existing customer to recommend you to a friend and persuade just one more customer to join you each year?

The business would start slowly, because you'd only have 128 customers after the first eight years. That might be OK in the construction industry or many consultancy businesses. It wouldn't be so good for a supermarket or a car manufacturer. But by the time you'd been going for 16 years, you would have 32,768 customers.

After 24 years, you'd have 8 million customers. After 34 years, you would be selling to every member of the human race. That's how it works. I admit it's a theoretical model and takes no account of deaths or distribution problems, but it really is worth thinking about.

Because the great truth that the world has lost sight of is simply this: customer retention is the key to success.

And the great news for smaller companies is that the financial muscle and limitless manpower of the biggest corporations are not going to give them the same overwhelming business advantages they've enjoyed in the past.

Those things were unstoppable when business was played according to 20th-century rules. In the 21st century, the rules of the game have changed.

Throughout the second half of the 20th century, victory went to those companies that could afford to use mass media

surely depends on product?

and mass media advertising to promote their brands and drag in more and more first-time customers. The Fords and the Vodafones, the Nikes and Unilevers, the Microsofts and Nokias – they just had to flex their financial biceps and the battle was won.

Now it's different. The mass media that favoured the big battalions have fragmented, splintered into a thousand pieces. In Malaysia, we used to have a handful of commercial TV channels and a couple of national newspapers. Hurl a big enough advertising budget at those obvious targets and you could guarantee to keep recruiting new buyers. Now there are hundreds of television channels, millions of websites and shoals of smaller, more localised or specialised papers and magazines, and no-one can afford the blanket coverage that used to be possible.

Attracting customers has become more difficult. But where focusing on customer retention used to be seen as a defensive tactic, the penny has finally dropped that retaining happy, profitable customers who will recommend you to others is much more than that. As US public relations expert Peter Shankman put it a couple of years ago, 'Take care of the customers you have and they'll bring you the customers you want.'

Retention has become the crucial factor in growing your business. And the only way to retain customers, in the face of aggressive competition, is to build a brand that they will recognise, trust, like and keep buying into.

If you get it right, those customers will happily share their interactions with the brand with all their real and digital friends. They will also develop a resilient and durable relationship with the brand. For example, most of them will be willing to forgive you the occasional mistake, as long as you recognise what's gone wrong, apologise sincerely and move fast to put things right.

The most obvious example of this kind of resilient relationship is the community of Apple Mac users. Almost without exception, people who have had Macs refuse to contemplate buying from anyone else. Every one of them has had problems from time to time, and every Mac user is all too familiar with the rainbow wheel of death, but that seems to make no dent in people's absolute loyalty to the brand. If a Mac breaks down, the usual response from an Apple owner is to shrug and mutter 'It'd be doing this every week if it was a PC.' And the global Mac community is so strong that a few seconds Googling is enough to find answers to almost any problem other than a complete mechanical failure.

The company's own customer service support has always been particularly good, but this is effectively amplified, free of charge, by a vast army of customers keen to share their tips, experiences and advice. The community itself adds real value for the customer, so that Apple actually benefits from the experiences of its customers' past problems. While its major competitors have spent billions, year after year, on increasingly lavish advertising campaigns, Apple has spent a fraction of that money, concentrating mainly on creating a genuine and well-understood Apple culture and spreading it far and wide across the ecosystem of customers, developers and business partners.

For other brands, which can only envy the ferocious loyalty Apple has generated over the years, the overall principle still holds. Resilient relationships are the only reliable defence against defections when a product disappoints or a service lets customers down. People won't put up with mistakes indefinitely, but most customers who have bought into the brand will still tend to be forgiving, at least the first time round.

A high proportion of any group of unhappy customers will always be buyers who were previously positive but have been upset by a single poor experience. These RUs – 'recently unhappies' – are a key target for action, as they are likely to be eyeing up your competitors and may even be on the point of taking their business elsewhere.

Ideally, for the sake of the brand, you want to be able to identify them fast and make amends as soon as possible. That's why the Ritz-Carlton hotel group has long had a policy of allowing employees to spend up to US$2,000, immediately and without prior authorisation, to compensate disgruntled customers and get them back on side.

There is strong research evidence to show that successfully solving problems in quick and generous ways that surprise and delight customers does more than just restore their faith in the brand. Remember the BA survey I quoted earlier: 'friendly and caring' service was the priority customers valued above all others. Owning up to mistakes and coming up with an appropriate and generous response actually deepens their commitment and virtually guarantees that they will become effective ambassadors for the brand.

Nick Wreden, one of the world's leading experts on the future of brands and branding, tells the story of UPS and the lost moon map as a wonderful example of how going the extra hundred miles won back an influential customer.

UPS had an important customer, the chairman of a major banking group, whose private passion was collecting maps. In a moment of inspiration, this man bought a very high quality map of the moon's surface and sent it off, in turn, to every one of the Apollo astronauts who had landed on the moon, asking each of them to sign it at the spot where he had walked on the lunar surface. Over a period of months, he collected almost all the signatures, right down to that of Eugene Cernan of Apollo 17, the twelfth and last man ever to set foot on the moon.

The final autograph he needed was that of Neil Armstrong. When he eventually agreed and added his signature, the collection was complete, and Armstrong sent the map back to the banker via UPS. But the carrier lost the package, and the banker suddenly became a very unhappy customer indeed.

The autographed map was effectively irreplaceable and the banker was distraught. The parcel was gone and there seemed to be nothing the courier could do to make up for its mistake. But one determined UPS customer service manager decided to make this his personal customer recovery mission. He bought a similarly high resolution moon map and began politely pestering every one of the astronauts all over again, explaining the circumstances, apologising for bothering them and begging each of them to sign once more. One by one by one they responded to his pleas, until eventually the second map was also signed by every human being who had ever set foot in the lunar dust and UPS was able to present the replacement map to its amazed and delighted ex-customer.

This man's influential position at the top of a major US banking group undoubtedly made it easier for UPS to justify a big and expensive effort to get him back. But many errors that upset or disappoint customers can be righted with relatively little effort or at low cost.

In Britain, the John Lewis/Waitrose group has built a mighty reputation as the most trusted retailer in the country, mainly by handling a host of routine, day-to-day problems, repairs and refunds quickly, politely and conscientiously. Even very price-conscious customers will buy from John Lewis, reassured by its 90-year-old 'Never knowingly undersold' promise and confident that the retailer's own customer service is likely to be more use than the manufacturer's guarantee if something goes wrong.

Turning 'recently unhappies' into satisfied customers with good things to say about the company has given John Lewis a competitive advantage no other British retailer can match. But there are some customers who will never be satisfied.

There's a specialist term we use here to refer to those

awkward customers who are never happy but never go away. We call them 'grumplers'. Every business has seen examples of grumplers among its customers. They are the high-maintenance individuals and companies that always have some complaint about your product, pricing, delivery or support services, but just keep on buying from you anyway. Often, they are so demanding and expensive to serve that you'd be better off if they switched to the competition. But they just won't go.

Getting rid of unprofitable customers to improve the bottom line was a hot business school and marketing media topic a few years ago. Several books and dozens of articles were published, all urging companies to be prepared to 'fire' resource-intensive customers who did not buy their more profitable products. Many different techniques for dealing with these perpetually dissatisfied customers were proposed, from unbundling packages so that overdemanding users had to pay directly for the support services they kept requiring to simply sending out notices terminating service agreements. This rather crude approach was adopted by a fair number of financial services and mobile phone companies, but often had undesirable consequences, including bad press and furious complaints on social media that caused serious damage to the brands involved.

These days the blanket enthusiasm for this 'customer divestment' has waned a little. It still makes sense to weed out customers that are blatantly abusing your services, unless they are also making an obvious contribution to profits. But in less clear-cut cases, it can be difficult to judge the trade-offs between the demands that are made and the direct and indirect value the customer brings.

Even an apparently unprofitable customer may be a great asset to the brand, if the relationship leads to recommendations and referrals or positive media coverage or allows you to develop convincing case studies. Young retail banking customers always cost the banks money in the short term, but have the potential to blossom into loyal and lucrative account holders as their careers progress. There are a lot of factors to take into account and finding the right data on individual customers presents its own challenges. So, given the cost and difficulty of recruiting new customers, the general rule of thumb must be to err on the side of keeping the customers you have.

This doesn't necessarily mean taking no action. The best approach, of course, is to turn unprofitable customers into profitable ones by selling them more units or a more profitable mix of products. Through the knowledge gleaned from your interactions with them, you may be able to suggest new areas where they could gain by buying different products or services from you. Alternatively, you may be able to increase margins by raising your prices – knowing that if your loss-making customer objects to the price hike and leaves, your profits will automatically improve. It's sometimes possible to reorganise services so that demanding or low-value customers are handled at lower cost using retail partners or distributors or online delivery channels. There are many different strategies that should be explored, and this is one area of customer retention that calls for real creative thinking.

In general, though, the rules for keeping customers are just what they have always been. It's all about winning the sale in the first place and then making sure your customers are pleasantly surprised to find they've got more for their money than they thought they were getting. It's about responding fast to queries, reacting fast to complaints and offering helpful advice and problem-solving support so that the customer benefits from the relationship.

All those things can potentially be done offline. But companies that organise themselves to deliver these benefits and build this relationship online can do it more efficiently, cheaper and often better, reaching out across a city, across a country or across the world. By making deft use of the internet and social media, they can nurture genuine two-way relationships that transcend geography and promote loyalty, building the brands that guarantee their future.

They can also preserve the ability to react fast to changing situations. We have moved away from the era when companies' brand strategies were based on major set-piece communications campaigns planned out 12 months or two years ahead and then doggedly executed as originally conceived. These days, that kind of rigid, unresponsive inflexibility is a recipe for disaster.

In our fast-changing business environment, nobody knows what new products, technologies and competitors are waiting round the corner. Prediction is useless, but preparation is all.

A strong brand prepares you for the unknown.

There's a lesson to be learned here from the grandmasters of the chess world. Even the finest players cannot analyse the whole game more than a few moves out. Garry Kasparov, possibly the greatest chess player of all time, once said he normally looked 'three to five moves' ahead. 'You don't need more,' he added.

For Kasparov and his rivals, both defence and attack are about seeing and reacting to what is happening around them. Much of their genius is built on strategic play, creating strong, flexible positions for themselves from which they can either defend against surprise assaults or make the most of unexpected opportunities.

That sounds to me like the ideal positioning for almost any 21st-century business. Building a brand is how you achieve it.

'Instead of the product taking centre stage, the individual customer should be at the heart of the process. Smart brands don't focus on the brand — they focus on the customer'

CHAPTER 7

Getting the Customer to Make the Sale

When my phone rang one evening, a couple of years ago, I quickly recognised the voice of Geoff H, chief executive of one of Malaysia's oldest-established insurance brokers.

I knew Geoff reasonably well, but we'd never done business before. And there was an urgency in his voice that told me this might be interesting.

'I want you to come over for a chat,' he said. 'This place needs a thorough shake-up, and I think Fusionbrand might be able to help us do it.'

On the way to the firm's office in the suburbs of Kuala Lumpur, I mulled over everything I knew about the business. It didn't add up to much.

I knew insurance broking was a highly regulated industry, and that Bank Negara Malaysia, the central bank, didn't allow brokers to do any advertising or conventional marketing. That would make it hard to generate the surge in new business Geoff was looking for.

I knew the firm had been around for years and its senior executives were widely respected. Its brand was well known, but tired, and finding ways to pull in new customers without breaking the strict Bank Negara rules was bound to be difficult.

But when we sat down to talk, it was clear the challenges were even more complicated than I'd guessed.

'We need to get the customer base growing again,' Geoff told me. 'But there's a whole new international angle to this, as well. We're trying to develop direct relationships with brokers at Lloyd's of London so we can try to work with Petronas, the national oil company. Those international boys will want to see a very different side of us from the side that will win us new customers here in Malaysia.'

So we talked, or rather I listened to Geoff as he gave me his insights into the company and how it worked. Geoff already trusted me and much of what he revealed must obviously remain confidential. But one of the first things he told me was that the company didn't have a website.

I was stunned. The firm would happily spend a fortune flying two or three top executives to London to meet Lloyd's of London brokers and try to form a relationship with them. But it hadn't invested in a website. The moment Geoff and his team left the shiny, futuristic Lloyd's building in the City of London, the people they had been talking to would turn straight to the internet to see what presence the firm had online and what others were saying about it. And what would they find? Nothing.

That was something that could be fixed. Creating a dynamic website with content that would resonate with prospects, customers and potential strategic partners like the London companies was a task I knew my team could handle readily enough. I knew we could give the firm an internet presence that would project a confident international image while still being bright, clear and relevant for potential customers here in Malaysia.

'No problem, Geoff,' I said. 'The website is not going to be all that difficult. But I think you're going to need a lot more than just a new website and an updated logo to get the business growing strongly.

'I'm pretty sure I know some of what's wrong, but give us a few days with your team and the contact numbers of some of your customers and other stakeholders and we'll find out a great deal more.'

My hunch was right. We worked out ten questions to open up key areas to talk about with the staff and different stakeholders and over the next few weeks we made phone calls and visited offices, taking every opportunity to capture the thoughts and perspectives of the firm's sales and customer service staff, as well as partners, suppliers, customers, past customers and even a few of the competitors these lost customers had defected to.

Internally, we reviewed the tools used to collect data, talked to staff and discussed how the firm gathered and analysed its customer data. We explored how that data was stored, mined, cleaned, added to, shared and used in sales or other branding areas. Although the firm can't advertise, it still communicates with customers and these communications were reviewed to determine whether the content was meaningful and relevant in the market segments the firm was targeting.

We also talked about staff members' individual perceptions of the brand and their understanding of the corporate values and how they applied to people's daily duties. Discussions were allowed to branch off at a tangent to explore other areas, and a lot of valuable insights resulted from these free-ranging digressions and detours.

Externally, we talked to various stakeholders about their interactions with the firm. When we talked to customers and lost customers, we asked about how well the broker had understood the customers' requirements for value. We also examined their perceptions of the ability of customer-facing staff members to empathise with them when providing advice or help and noted how well they felt the broker's front-line people had responded to their needs.

When Geoff and I got together again, I was able to sum it up.

'We need to do the obvious creative work – refreshing the logo and creating a website that will present a sophisticated and professional image to potential strategic partners and customers in the UK and elsewhere. But that's not the big task. The main challenge is to change the way your people think and work and represent your brand when they're with the customer.

'Once we've done that, we can look at raising your profile and positioning you as a thought leader in your industry. First, though, we need your people to be ready to deliver on every promise the brand makes.

'You're not going to like it, Geoff, because it'll take time and it'll mean investing in training and staff development, and maybe a certain amount of new technology. But I guarantee you it'll be paying off inside a year.'

To my surprise, Geoff didn't respond with a volley of verbal abuse.

'No. You're right,' he said. 'The chairman and I knew all that, really, Marcus. We just hadn't dared to admit it to ourselves. Let's get going and sort this firm out.'

While the designers set to work on updating the logo and creating an attractive, customer-friendly website with dynamic and SEO-tuned content that would attract spiders and ensure high search engine rankings, Geoff and I worked out what messages needed to be conveyed to the Lloyd's people in London. Apart from projecting a general air of confidence and competence, we decided it was vital to highlight the broad industry and international experience of the broker's key staff. It was also important – for both home and international audiences – to stress the firm's principles and integrity.

When we turned the full focus of our attention onto the issues of staff attitudes and customer service, we quickly realised that the poor impression some stakeholders had of the firm's performance and capabilities was not always due to individual staff members' lack of skills or effort. It was simply that Geoff's people had been pointed in the wrong direction – or, more likely, in the urgent quest for new business the firm just hadn't had the time or resources to invest in getting everyone on brand. The whole company had been focused on an old-fashioned features-driven selling approach that was all wrong for today's market.

I told Geoff that his staff needed to know more about their customers and potential customers. The firm needed more and better data, and the first step towards this was to adopt a customer relationship management *system that would bring together everything that was known about an individual or company and enable staff to use this information to maximum effect.*

The firm had never used a CRM system before, but we were soon able to plug that gap, using cloud-based software that required no extra hardware and involved very low upfront costs. Using the power of the integrated CRM approach, staff could get to know their customers better, collect their comments and feedback, improve the quality and consistency of all the firm's communications and sustain relationships that would prevent small issues from growing into major gripes.

More broadly, though, there needed to be a shift of focus, away from selling good but standardised insurance solutions and towards delivering value to customers, based on a thorough understanding of each customer's specific economic, experiential and emotional needs. This would change the nature of the relationship between the firm and its customers and help the firm begin to build a brand that would encourage loyalty and word-of-mouth recommendations. Instead of the product taking centre stage, the individual customer would be at the heart of the process.

That, of course, is how it has to be. Smart brands don't focus on the brand – they focus on the customer. Once the firm had taken this idea on board, it was ready to make a major change for the better.

Geoff and I set about changing the focus by training all the broker's customer-facing employees – from top to bottom – to understand that branding depended on delivering value and managing relationships from the customer's perspective. The brand, we explained, had little to do with logos and straplines and a slick and plausible website. It was not embodied in what the firm said, but in how it treated its customers and how they came to feel about it.

And because that was something that could be enhanced by every positive, thoughtful customer contact and harmed by every brusque or insensitive interaction with customers or potential customers, the future of the brand lay in the hands of every one of the broker's employees.

Geoff's people were quick to see the importance of this and made a real effort to change the way they dealt with sales and service situations and customer queries. Gradually, the firm became less of a conventional broker, selling standardised products, and more of a consultant and collaborator for its customers. Sales conversations focused on the fact that the broker worked for the customer, not the insurance company, and therefore had the customer's interests at heart. This was a key point, and spelling it out helped to reverse a long-term trend that had seen the firm losing increasing amounts of business to tied agents and insurance companies.

The goldmine of information captured in the CRM system also meant that staff were much better prepared, and could offer policies that were more specifically tailored to each customer's needs. The new information helped the broker's employees understand the individual customer's requirements better and, drawing on their own experience, predict the issues that might arise, so they could match policies more closely to the customer's needs. It also enabled staff to capture additional business by suggesting appropriate policy endorsements, exclusions and amendments before the customers even realised they'd be needed.

The results were spectacular. Twelve months later, nearly three-quarters of the broker's customers had responded by increasing their spend on insurance, and retention rates had soared. It was a vast improvement – and it had all been achieved without paying out for a single advertisement.

At the end of the first year, Geoff invited me over for another meeting.

'Come in, Marcus,' he said, smiling and gesturing towards a chart he had stuck up on the wall. 'Take a look at this. I've just got the figures. I think you'll be proud of what we've done.'

The graph showed a dramatic upward slope, starting around mid-year and climbing ever more steeply.

'These are our referral rates,' said Geoff. 'They're 39 per cent up on last year and still getting better every month. Don't you just love it when your customers go out and do your selling for you?'

'Brands will be made or broken at the point of contact with the customer, online or face to face. Flashy logos, smart slogans and massive advertising campaigns will no longer be enough to grab and hold your customers' interest'

CHAPTER 8

It's the People, Stoopid

In October 2014, one hundred of the UK's biggest companies woke up to find that *Which?*, a trusted and much-loved non-profit consumer magazine, had published a huge and detailed survey into what customers really thought about them. And a lot of the news wasn't very flattering.

When *Which?* speaks, people listen. Its consumer research and product testing is legendary and it always has the courage to name names and tell the uncomfortable truth about poor products and lousy performance.

So the results of this new survey were shocking. They showed that customer service really mattered – far more than most companies seem to realise – and that it was a major factor, right up there alongside price, value for money and product quality, in building and maintaining a brand.

The survey showed that some of Britain's biggest and most well-known companies, including major banks, phone companies, energy suppliers and retailers, were delivering truly terrible standards of service.

And it listed, more clearly than I have ever seen before, exactly what consumers found best and worst about the way companies treat them.

This is great information to have, because it provides a string of clues about how ambitious companies can improve the way staff interact with customers. The problems are just the same in Southeast Asia as they are in Britain, and this survey data is gold dust. If you know what customers' pet peeves are, you can do something about them.

Building a brand that customers will love, be loyal to and talk to others about is very largely to do with getting it right when your people are face to face with the customer. So here's how *not* to do it, straight from the horse's mouth, courtesy of *Which?* and more than 3,500 real consumers.

These are the things customers hate.

You'll recognise them, of course, because they are precisely the things *you* hate when you are in a shop or a showroom in Kuala Lumpur, Jakarta or Singapore or trying to get a query answered or a problem solved with your own bank, mobile operator or satellite TV provider:

- Rude staff
- Having to wait for service or to get a query answered
- Being ignored while staff talk among themselves
- Long queues
- Shop staff trying to sell you products you don't want
- Staff who don't know about the products they're selling

Just paying attention to these six points can go a long way towards making sure that your staff don't undermine your brand by treating customers badly. They are all problems that can be fixed fairly easily, if you are determined enough, simply by making sure you employ the right people, train them properly and put the right procedures and processes in place to steer them towards doing a good job every day.

But even more important, I believe, is letting them know what you want them to do and how you want them to be when they are in contact with your precious customers. Some individuals can never be turned into great customer service staff. But most people can be helped to raise their game, and good training and organisation, with clear goals and proper rewards, can make all the difference.

Getting it right starts with a clear understanding of what currently happens when customers are in contact with your staff. That's why it is so important to begin with the careful, unglamorous work of carrying out a comprehensive brand healthcheck (*see Chapter 20 – What Is Your Brand Really Saying?*). This is a detailed audit exercise that looks at what actually goes on, rather than what people think or say they do. Once you know that, you can start to make the changes – often surprisingly small adjustments – that are needed to make your staff a major plus factor in building a great brand.

Which? is a tremendously respected research organisation, but it is based in the UK and, of course, the people it interviewed were in the UK, too. After 21 years living here in Malaysia, I felt that everything about the customers' responses to the *Which?* survey questions rang true for me. But I still knew it would be a mistake to assume that the same factors would be equally important in different cultures and different markets.

Would consumers in Southeast Asia feel the same way? Would the same things irritate and frustrate them, or would their expectations of customer service be different?

Instinct and experience told us the answers would probably be much the same. But there is no substitute for proper field research, so we decided to mobilise the Fusionbrand team and ask consumers in Kuala Lumpur, Singapore and Jakarta the same questions.

The results were startlingly similar. People in this part of the world were just as annoyed by poor service, couldn't-care-less attitudes and lack of product knowledge. They hated it when staff kept them waiting unnecessarily and talked among themselves. And, like shoppers in the UK, they strongly resented clumsy attempts to sell them products or services they did not want.

The big difference – especially noticeable in Malaysia and Singapore – was that they reacted to poor treatment in a different way.

The UK has become a society of activist consumers, and many people there are quite happy, these days, to make their complaints very public, using Facebook, Twitter, TripAdvisor and other social media to name and shame the companies that don't treat them right.

If they don't get satisfaction, they will often email the company, write to the CEO or make their voices heard on consumer watchdog programmes on local or national radio stations. In some cases, they will even go along to the company's AGM and kick up a fuss to get their problems solved.

In Southeast Asia, it seems, customers just vote with their feet.

They walk out of the store, cancel subscriptions or switch brands. But they don't often air their dissatisfaction in public – not yet, anyway. As a result, companies that undermine their own brands by treating customers badly or providing poor service and support simply don't have any idea who or how many people they have offended and how much business they've lost.

In fact, if they are still managing to attract a flow of new customers, the defection of their old customers may be largely masked, until it is too late and permanent damage is done to the brand.

We all know – even if we don't like to admit it out loud – that our local retailers, in particular, have a hard time competing with their big international rivals. Our shopping malls are completely dominated by Marks & Spencer, Isetan, Uniqlo and the rest. They have the big names and the big bucks on their side, and, historically, this has always been enough to put them in pole position. But branding – real, engaging, open, human, customer-centred branding – offers our smaller regional retailers the best opportunity yet to turn the tables on these overseas giants.

So what can a company in Southeast Asia do to make sure its front-line staff build and strengthen its brand, rather than weakening it?

Based on our own research and the work *Which?* did in the UK, it's easy enough to put together a checklist of elements you should pay attention to. Simply making sure you get these things right will guarantee you a place near the upper end of any customer service rating scale.

Focusing on this short list of priorities provides a real opportunity for companies to differentiate themselves and make customers love them, just by setting extraordinarily high standards for every customer interaction. This is an area where small firms have a potential advantage, because of their more personal nature and shorter chains of command. Big organisations often know perfectly well that they should be doing it, too, but they always struggle to come to terms with the detail of these human factors.

In practice, the key points are:

1. Employ the right people, with the right attitudes and enthusiasm
2. Stop promoting people just because of their long service, or at least move those without the right skills into roles that are out of the front line
3. Train customer-facing staff thoroughly, both in terms of product training and developing their people skills
4. Set up rewards or bonus schemes that provide incentives for the kind of behaviour and performance you really want. Instead of relying on crude, antiquated commission schemes

that reward sales and ignore relationships, you should be looking at metrics like customer interactions and retention and shares and comments on Facebook and other social media communities. It's all about value now, not transactions.

5. Make sure your staff have the processes, tools, product knowledge and access to information they need to do a good job, plus the authority to act on their own initiative

These will be radical changes for many Asian companies. But they are the necessary foundations, if you are going to build a brand that customers will embrace. What's more, new systems and technologies have added another imperative that is completely new.

Today, you need to know about your customers as individuals and treat them like that. This is a new factor, and it calls for a completely new mindset, backed up by the use of a number of new technologies.

What has changed abruptly in the last few years is the ability to collect data about your customers and use it in fresh and imaginative ways. Good customer service is no longer just a matter of relying on the face-to-face skills of individual sales people. These days, it needs to be backed up by retail systems that help and support their efforts.

For example, when a customer pulls out his loyalty card, your retail system should immediately provide the sales person with a clear view of that customer's past purchases, spending and history with the company. This is valuable information, because it equips your people with important clues that will help them do the right things, such as spotting opportunities for cross-selling and upselling and for working with customers to develop them into brand advocates.

But this is only the beginning. The problem with loyalty cards is that they only come into play when the customer is already at the till and about to complete a purchase.

Ideally, of course, what's needed is some sort of system that will deliver this kind of real-time customer profiling when customers first come into the store, rather than when they have already made up their minds to make a purchase or have lost interest and started to drift away. And the good news is that this kind of system is already on its way.

In the next few years, technology and branding will come together to improve both the shopper's experience and the retailer's ability to match the offering to the customer in wholly new ways.

The big change will be that the retailer's system will be automatically triggered by a signal from the customer's smartphone as he or she walks into the shop. This will tell your sales staff immediately – via screens on the counter or the tablets most front-line people will soon be carrying – whether the person who has just come in is a first-time visitor or an existing customer. If the system recognises a customer who has bought from you before, it will help these front-line staff know straight away which products or areas of interest are most likely to be relevant to this individual.

This is not science fiction. Nor is it some pie-in the-sky vision that we won't see till 2030. Similar technologies to this are already being tested in the United States and Britain.

Visitors to shopping malls who are walking past a specialist wine store or a supermarket will be pinged with special one-off offers specifically targeted at them and their preferred products. So there will be a special offer on the customer's favourite French wine or the particular cheese or coffee this person has chosen before, and it will pop up at just the right moment on the customer's smartphone.

Consumers have to be given the ability to opt out easily from this kind of push marketing, but large-scale trials have shown that many welcome it and find it helpful, rather than intrusive, in this kind of retailing context.

Other ingenious ways of bringing the product and the customer together are in the pipeline – some initiated by the brand owner, some by the retailer.

Before long, customers will be able to choose to register with their favourite brands, so that wherever they are doing their shopping – locally or even in another country – the relevant retailers will be able to present them with appropriate offers.

Waitrose, the most upmarket of all the UK supermarket chains, has already launched a revolutionary scheme that gives its myWaitrose loyalty card holders a 20 per cent discount on their favourite products whenever they shop in the store or online. What's unique about the idea is that each individual card holder can choose which ten products in his or her basket will be discounted. These personalised, customer-selected discounts are then triggered automatically, thanks to the company's sophisticated computer systems, whenever the card holder shops at Waitrose.

Developments like this are going to be crucial to the future of brands, for manufacturers, service companies and retailers. Brands will be made or broken at the point of contact with the customer, online or face to face. Flashy logos, smart slogans and copy lines and massive advertising campaigns will no longer be enough to grab and hold your customers' interest.

We won't see many more examples of the sort of ill-thought-out launches we are used to in Southeast Asia, where a company like, say, Gap, spends millions of dollars fitting out new stores, rolling out a big ad campaign and bringing in some big-name mainland Chinese celebrity for a lavish opening ceremony, only to undo the good work by staffing its outlets with nervous, untrained 18-year-olds who can't hold a proper conversation with the sort of customers who come through the doors.

The penny is starting to drop. Branding is about

relationships – building a relationship with the customer that feels positive, helpful and engaging.

It's about making the customer feel involved in a two-way process, with benefits to both sides, that is not only about maximising short-term profit for the company. It's about recognising that each customer's individual requirements may be different, and nurturing a dialogue that acknowledges those differences and makes a real effort to accommodate them. Despite the growing role of behind-the-scenes systems and technologies, at the customer touchpoint, it is about people.

The *Which?* report that Britain's biggest companies found so disturbing should not have come as a surprise to them.

They should have known – without needing a survey to tell them – that their brands were at risk if their people were rude, lazy, ill-informed, offhand or unhelpful. And since customer reactions in KL, Singapore and Jakarta seem to be much the same as those in London, Leeds and Glasgow, we, too, need to pay close attention to the people we hire and the way we train, equip and incentivise them if we are to build robust, engaging, profitable brands in the increasingly sophisticated and competitive markets of Southeast Asia.

'What we need is a simple, rugged tool that can help us back our winners and stop chasing losers.

I like RFM. It always seems like a good way of utilising business judgement in a controlled framework, and it works for small firms as well as big ones'

CHAPTER 9

What's That Customer Worth to You?

One CEO I worked with – let's call him Mr Lee – had a big international customer called XYZ Corp. Mr Lee liked the big cheques that came in from XYZ. But the cheques were always late and the customer's disregard for deadlines meant Mr Lee often had to pay overtime. XYZ needed a lot of handholding, monopolising the Asian company's service desk, making unscheduled requests for tech support and often calling day-long meetings that seemed to achieve nothing at all.

Another customer, ABC, generated just 20% of the sales XYZ did. But ABC made far fewer demands. Bills were paid promptly, deadlines were honoured and the only support that was needed was a service call once or twice a year. ABC was unglamorous, but clearly a profitable customer.

On the other hand, Mr Lee's gut feeling told him XYZ was more trouble than it was worth. The revenue was welcome, but was XYZ actually profitable, once all the costs of servicing the account were factored in? It was hard to know for sure…

Everyone believes in valuing the customer. But how many Asian businesses set about seriously trying to find out what their customers are really worth to them? Remarkably few, to be honest.

The problem is that the true value of a new customer – the

total value of the relationship over its entire lifetime – is not just the profit you can make from providing a succession of purchases and services.

To be completely realistic, any number you arrive at must also reflect more intangible contributions, such as the marketing value of recommendations and referrals and positive word-of-mouth comment. Suggestions and even criticisms from a trusted customer can be immensely valuable in developing and fine tuning new products. And if you win a large or respected business as a customer, the very fact that you are a supplier to such a company can be a major marketing asset, boosting your credibility and your perceived stature in the market.

There are three or four common ways of calculating the lifetime value of a customer, though they all require a bit of subjective guesswork when it comes to representing these slippery intangibles. But you have to start somewhere – as Nick Wreden, author of the excellent *ProfitBrand: How to Increase the Profitability, Accountability and Sustainability of Brands*, has always insisted.

'When it comes to calculating lifetime customer value, it is better to be approximately right than exactly wrong,' says Wreden, echoing a famous line from the economist JM Keynes.

Wreden's book quotes examples of customer value calculations that begin by totalling up the direct sales revenues and then add in an extra 5 per cent for the value of the intangible spin-offs. Scoring the intangibles at 3 per cent is more common and probably nearer the mark, but 3 percentage points either way is certainly the sort of variation that could make a lot of difference to a company's overall profit margin.

The most basic way of calculating customer value involves multiplying the average sale per customer by the number of times the average customer buys in a year and then multiplying that by the number of years your customer continues to buy.

Average sale per customer is simply your sales revenue divided by the number of customers you have. You can divide your total number of invoices for the year by the number of customers to find out how often your average customer buys. The dates in your customer records will make it easy to calculate an average figure for how long customers stay with you, from the first purchase to the last, though the figures will be badly skewed if you don't make sure to include past customers as well as your present clientele.

So, on this basis, customer equity = average sale x annual purchases x duration (in years) of the sales relationship.

Doing this kind of rough-and-ready sum will help you and your staff understand how much is lost when a customer leaves. That can be useful in directing people's attention to the importance of customer retention. But this approach does have its weaknesses. In particular, it averages everything out and makes no distinction between a dream customer and one that is awkward, expensive to serve and possibly even unprofitable. It doesn't factor in costs, either, so there is nothing here that relates to profit, rather than volume.

Another favourite quick-and-dirty technique is a retention-based customer equity calculation. This requires you to know your year-to-year retention rate – the percentage of your customers that you succeed in holding onto from year to year. But that is available more often than you might think. Many companies that are generally very short of detailed financial information can still quote you a customer retention rate, possibly because this is a number that sales people like to have at their fingertips when negotiating their pay and bonuses.

To do a retention-based customer equity calculation, you begin by simply totalling up all sales to new customers and dividing by the number of new customers you have acquired. This will give you a figure for the average sale to a first year customer.

You might have, for example, 500 new customers each spending US$5,000. This will add up to a Year One total of US$2.5m. If your retention rate is 70 per cent, this generation of customers will contribute US$1.75m in Year Two and only US$1.225m in Year Three. If the actual retention rate is low, the effect of attrition is quite stark. If retention falls to 60 per cent, for example, the contribution from those 500 new customers will go down sharply from US$2.5m in Year One to US$1.5m in Year Two and less than a million in Year Three.

If you do these sums over the period you have identified as the average customer lifetime, you can calculate the gross cumulative sales to this generation of customers, subtract the acquisition costs for this group and divide by the original number of Year One recruits, giving you a figure for the average lifetime value of a customer.

This method is also pretty approximate, but it does begin to reflect some of the cost side of the equation, through allowing for the initial marketing spend. (There are ongoing costs associated with every customer, of course, but these fall dramatically after the first purchase.)

Exceptions – very good and very bad customers – remain averaged out and hidden in the mix, but showing how customers become more profitable the longer they stay is certainly a powerful way of illustrating the crucial importance of retention rates. Improving retention rates by just one or two percentage points quickly makes a big difference to the total value you can derive from your customer base.

The standard 'official' method of calculating customer lifetime value is more accurate and more complex and is therefore done less often and understood by fewer people. Thinking back to Nick Wreden and JM Keynes, there's probably a lot to be said for a back-of-an-envelope approach that people can actually use to get somewhere near the truth, rather than more comprehensive and exacting processes that require statistical expertise and will only occasionally be used. For customer lifetime value calculations, near enough is good enough.

The standard customer equity formula requires you to:

MULTIPLY retained customers x average sales per customer

ADD a suitable allowance (3% to 5%) for referrals and other indirect value

SUBTRACT cost of goods, cost to serve and overheads allocated to customers

DISCOUNT for Net Present Value★ to reflect the lower value of tomorrow's money

SUBTRACT acquisition (marketing) costs

This formula gives you a figure for total customer equity, which is divided by the original number of customers to tell you what a new customer should be worth.

You can go further still in this direction, towards the creation of a 'customer P&L' for each buyer. This involves allocating a share of process costs, including manpower, transport and handling and support costs, and even costs of capital. This is the Rolls-Royce, the gold standard of customer equity calculations. It takes a lot of data and a lot of work, but there are some companies that have made this precise knowledge of customer value and profitability into a powerful source of competitive advantage.

Wreden found the example of US trucker Roadway Express, which uses spreadsheets and customer P&Ls to cost every activity for every customer, so that it can tell immediately whether any particular order is going to be profitable.

After starting to do this, Roadway quite deliberately declined 350,000 tons of haulage work in a single year, driving its sales down but sending its profits soaring by sidestepping unprofitable assignments. In an industry that runs on tight

2.5 per cent margins, this single improvement to the way it did business raised Roadway's revenue per ton by 4 per cent. Knowing exactly which services for which customers were profitable meant Roadway's managers could also plot a very clear path to future profit growth.

Many businesses will feel they don't need to calculate the precise numbers around lifetime customer value, let alone the full details of a customer P&L.

What they do need is the ability to identify valuable customers, so they can be nurtured, and to spot low-value customers that will never repay the sales, marketing and support efforts needed to reach and service them. These are relative, rather than absolute, values, but knowing the relative importance of your customers is usually what matters most.

So back in the rough and ready world that most of us do business in, what we need is a simple, rugged tool that can help us back our winners and stop chasing losers. And there is one less demanding and less arithmetical approach to recognising which customers really count that any business can use. It's known as RFM. I like RFM. It always seems like a good way of utilising business judgement in a controlled framework, and it works for small firms as well as big ones.

RFM stands for Recency, Frequency and Monetary Value. It doesn't actually quantify customer value, but it can be a powerful tool for helping you recognise it. RFM was originally developed for use in direct mail, way back in the 1930s, and it's based on some sound commonsense principles. It scores customers on the basis of how recently they have bought, how often they have bought and how much they have spent.

Customers who have bought recently are more likely to buy again than those who haven't, and hence are scored higher. Customers who buy frequently tend to keep coming back. And those who spend more money are also more likely to return. There you have it. RFM. There is actually good evidence to back up these working assumptions, including research that shows that a customer that makes three purchases in fairly quick succession is twice as likely to become a long-term customer.

The system works by scoring each customer on a scale of 1 to 5 for recency, then for frequency and then for monetary value. You set the scales yourself, in whatever terms seem most significant to your business. You might, for example, decide that, as far as recency was concerned, 1 meant a customer that had bought a year ago and 5 meant a customer that had bought in the last month. In an industry where deals were bigger and slower, you might make 1 represent a purchase more than five years ago and 5 stand for a purchase in the past year. The point is that these are relative, rather than absolute scores. But that does not mean they are useless.

In fact, they can be very helpful. Each of your customers ends up with a three-digit score, somewhere between 555 (best of the best for recency and frequency and value) and 111 (pretty uninspiring all round). So a customer that scored 1 for recency, 3 for frequency and 4 for monetary value would have a score of 134. The digits would actually be rearranged so that the highest comes first, so this customer would be shown as 431, making it very simple to stack customers in ranking order from highest down to lowest.

At its simplest, RFM helps you identify where to focus your marketing effort. But it can be used in other ways, too. If you do the same exercise every six months and see a customer's score rising or falling, that trend can show you whether the customer's potential value to you is going up or down.

A falling RFM score also means that the customer is becoming more likely to defect to a competitor. Some companies use RFM as a trigger or tripwire, so that a score that falls below, say, 322 automatically prompts a sales call, a contact via email or Facebook or some other action to save the situation.

RFM can help your business do better. One of its great advantages is precisely the fact that it is simple. If you are in a business that has 200 customers, rather than 200,000, you can do the whole thing manually, at no cost other than an hour or two's effort. Yet it can help you segment your customers in ways that bring direct and profitable results.

Nick Wreden quotes the case of a UK catalogue company selling music CDs and audio books to a base of 250,000 customers. Simply segmenting this customer base, using RFM, and retargeting its marketing efforts enabled the company to raise sales by 5 per cent. Another way to raise revenue by 5 per cent would have been to recruit an extra 12,500 new customers, but that would obviously have involved a lot more effort, investment and risk. RFM can give you quick wins, whether you are a large corporation or a small family business.

For the big boys, RFM can become a very sophisticated business tool that draws on vast amounts of data and calls for a lot of computing power. Multinationals like FedEx use their own customised versions of RFM, coding all their customers according to their RFM cells and then keeping a careful (computerised) eye on customers migrating from cell to cell. FedEx has adapted the basic RFM approach to its own needs, using a 1 to 10 scale rather than 1 to 5, for example, to help it pick up smaller movements. It used the modified RFM approach to group customers into seven 'clusters' and tracked the patterns of migration over two years. The results were extremely useful.

FedEx found that it had a stable, loyal and profitable Top 10 per cent – key customers that were worth almost any effort to keep on board. But it also identified a small group it called 'growing, high-value' customers. These were each worth just a third as much as the Top 10 per cent customers, but their potential was phenomenal. They were growing fast, with a 1,500 per cent increase in monetary value over a two-year period, and stood out as prime targets for FedEx marketing efforts.

The segmentation exercise also produced other valuable insights. It helped identify seasonal businesses that only used FedEx at certain times of the year. Focusing the marketing push on the relevant season meant every dollar in this area could achieve much better results.

'Migration clusters' became a marketing buzzword at FedEx and the key to making the most of a large, but not infinite, marketing budget. In the last three or four years, it has become a key element in helping FedEx management develop better investment strategies and more relevant marketing messages.

This kind of advanced, dynamic RFM migration analysis is obviously too complicated for many businesses, but even the basic, static, rough-and-ready RFM can deliver impressive results. If you are not already doing it, you should consider trying it out now.

In the past, people were sometimes worried that individual RFM scores could occasionally be misleading. The awkward, distant customer who was always putting in small orders for your lowest-margin products could come out as a heroic 551, though he might actually be costing you money and be a strong candidate for being dropped altogether. But most managers will be able to think of ways to find or filter out these false heroes without too much trouble, leaving a ranking – and a perspective – that is valuable, robust and easily understood by everybody in the business.

★ *Net Present Value (NPV) is based on the principle that a dollar today is worth more than one tomorrow. The basis for the decline in value over time is the discount rate, which is often equal to the inflation rate but may also take into account the risk associated with an investment. The NPV of US$1,000 with a discount rate of 10% would be about US$909 after one year, US$826 after two years and just US$751 after three years.*

'If the people who work for an organisation don't have a clear and shared understanding of what the brand means, there is no chance they will be able to engage with the outside world'

CHAPTER 10

Vision Plus Detail:
100+ Steps to Build a Brand

What stops organisations building successful brands, even when they have substantial budgets, something important to say and something interesting to sell?

It's a key question, and there are as many different answers as there are underperforming brands.

But one vital factor that certainly makes it impossible to create and sustain a strong and profitable brand is a lack of clarity.

If you don't know who you are, why you're there, what you are trying to do and communicate and how you want to be perceived, you cannot hope to get your branding right.

I saw a prime example of this recently when Fusionbrand successfully tendered for a large branding project with a Malaysian government agency which had recently undergone a major management shake-up and been through an agonising period of self-examination. The agency issued invitations to tender because it wanted to understand perceptions of its brand and get an outside perspective on the brand and the effectiveness of its communications.

In my opinion, formal tenders offer an entirely reasonable and well-established process for awarding contracts for big, concrete projects like major IT systems or building a school or a road, where materials, components and labour are always going to account for a large part of the price. But they are not necessarily the best way to go about choosing a supplier in an area like branding, where what's needed is understanding, insight and creativity.

This project seemed interesting and challenging, though, so we were prepared to go along with the selection process and jump through all the necessary hoops. Starting with a list of a dozen companies – ad agencies, PR firms and one or two of the more specialised branding consultancies we would see as our direct competitors – the agency gradually whittled the contenders down to a shortlist, culminating in a three-way pitch for the business.

We won the contract, on the basis of our experience, ideas, reputation and, probably, price. But as soon as we began the communications audit which forms the essential starting point for any serious branding work, we quickly found that we had a major task on our hands.

The agency – which, unfortunately, for reasons of customer confidentiality, cannot be identified here – had been established about eight years earlier. It had had some notable successes, but the Malaysian government felt that it had failed to make the overall impact, at home and abroad, that it should have been able to make. It was operating in a fast-expanding field where there was an obvious need for the advice, technical knowhow and market expertise it could provide. Yet, somehow, it had not managed to put its message across to the wide range of businesses and other organisations it was set up to help – and aggressive competition from Thailand and the UK was threatening its position as the best in the business.

Even before we began our research into how the agency was seen by its customers, suppliers and other external stakeholders, we found clear evidence of confusion among the organisation's own employees about what its aims were and what its branding was trying to achieve.

For example, when we asked the agency's staff 'What is our branding goal?', the answers ranged far and wide.

Some employees talked about promoting investment, setting standards and raising awareness. Others said it was all about publicising and co-ordinating the development of the industry.

Some thought it was about encouraging a healthy lifestyle, but some of their colleagues were equally convinced that the brand's goal was to help Malaysian companies find export opportunities in the wider global market.

'Providing consumers with awareness, information and education and training,' said one agency employee, while another, obviously frustrated and disenchanted with the slow progress the agency was making, gave the most negative answer of all.

Asked 'What is our branding goal?', this disgruntled staff member replied 'None.'

These widely scattered views of what the brand was meant to be doing and representing had obviously made it difficult for the employees to work together in a unified and consistent way.

If the people who work for an organisation don't have a clear and shared understanding of what the brand means, there is no chance they will be able to engage with the outside world. In this case, millions of dollars were being spent every year on conventional marketing activities – brochures, advertisements, websites and exhibitions – with no single, coherent message and very little return to show for the money that was invested. Much of the content didn't resonate with the target markets and there were no processes or systems in place to follow up and engage the leads generated by these activities.

Indeed, the next stage of our background research, exploring customers' views of the agency and its activities, uncovered plenty of negative reactions.

'Slow to respond' was a common theme, alongside criticisms of poor communication and unsatisfactory customer service. Some customers were obviously impressed with what the agency was doing, but there were enough negative comments to make it clear that the internal confusion about what the brand stood for was undermining much of the good work.

In today's world, where a brand's meaning is largely determined by the reaction of its customers and other stakeholders to physical and digital experiences, rather than by the messages pumped out by its marketing department, the attitudes and behaviour of every member of *staff are vitally important. Living the brand is the key to success, but how can employees live the brand if they don't know what it is supposed to mean?*

The early stages of our brand communication audit made it very clear that the internal brand communication programme was not working properly. People were too focused on their day-to-day tasks to spare much of a thought for the brand. The agency, as a whole, was suffering from the fact that every member of staff had a different view of the brand's values and priorities and from the organisation's inability to sum up its meaning and purpose in one consistent message.

As we delved deeper and looked at the way the agency had been spending its marketing dollars to build its brand, a similar picture of fragmented, unco-ordinated activity emerged.

Some of the individual initiatives were well handled, but people who were given the agency's glossy corporate brochures at seminars, exhibitions and conferences, for example, were receiving information that was actually two years out of date. The content hadn't been updated. In this dynamic and quickly changing environment, two-year-old information is history. The fact that it was embedded in expensively designed and superficially impressive brochures only served to confuse potential customers about the agency's current schemes and capabilities – and to raise awkward questions about how their tax dollars were being spent.

The website, the first port of call for most people who want to find out about the agency's work, was clumsy and anything but inviting and interactive. Page after page carried slabs of heavyweight text that had all too obviously been cut and pasted from print documents, ignoring the fact that web copy must always be crisp and succinct, because it is read in a completely different way.

Any paragraph that runs to more than three lines looks dull and off-putting on the web and the agency's pages ignored the basic rules about breaking up information into bite-sized chunks, using headings and subheads to provide visual pointers and deploying pictures and diagrams intelligently. There were also aspects of the web experience that looked as if they might have been designed to deter people from registering to receive further information – including the requirement, on sign-up, to give not just an email address and a name but a passport or MyKad ID number as well.

At the more detailed level, we found that employees' business cards used many different designs and fonts and carried different and sometimes apparently conflicting information. Customer names and contact details that were collected at exhibitions and face-to-face events were not used for any follow-up communications. Every advertising campaign seemed to have a different focus and a different look and feel, and we found one ad in an important international business magazine that did not even offer a web address or any contact details for the agency.

Simply imposing more discipline across all these activities and paying more attention to the detail of their execution offered the opportunity to make considerable improvements and substantial savings. But I was concerned that we should take the process a lot further than that. And we still had more digging to do before we could start to suggest a way forward that would produce the results the agency should have been getting from its US$2 million branding and marketing budget.

We needed to find out more about what the agency's external stakeholders thought of it. So we created an online survey aimed at consumers, business customers (ranging in size from SMEs to global giants like Nestlé and Kelloggs), suppliers and people in government. This was revealing in many different ways, as each of these constituencies seemed to have run into different issues and challenges in its dealings with the agency – lots of them relating to offhand, careless or incompetent treatment by agency staff.

Many suppliers, for example, complained that the agency had lost their goodwill by paying bills late, for no apparent reason. Government officials felt they had been given the wrong information for their purposes. And customers, again, bemoaned the agency's lack of responsiveness and inability to provide the kind of support they had hoped for and expected.

We were working on this contract with two of the top managers in the agency's communications division. The initial scope of the project had involved brand and communications audits and the production of a two-year communications plan, but it quickly became obvious that the agency was keen to take a broader, more holistic view of its branding. We set about producing a series of recommendations and specific actions that could be taken, within the limits of existing budgets, to revitalise the brand and position it for future growth.

The result was a list of more than a hundred recommendations, ranging from immediate actions that would lead to quick wins to longer-term strategic initiatives.

In the quick wins category, we recommended revising stationery, presentation and business card formats to present a consistent look and brand image. We proposed automating online forms so that the information entered flowed directly into the agency's database, improving the quality and style of all promotional merchandise and beefing up the content quality and look of leaflets, booklets and brochures.

On the digital front, we suggested making the agency's digital apps more useful and customer-friendly and putting in place a far more engaging and interactive Facebook presence, with regularly updated content, plenty of space for posts from visitors and proper, prompt and personalised engagement with every visitor comment.

All of these tactical recommendations – and many more – could be followed up quickly and relatively inexpensively, laying the foundations for action at a more strategic level.

Our major strategic proposals included:

1. Defining and clarifying internal goals and improving training to shift the organisational culture towards greater engagement and collaboration with customers
2. Placing a new emphasis on the localisation of products and marketing
3. Creating new branding goals and specific milestones to measure customer engagement, relationship development and social media conversations

4. *Showing employees and customers how to become brand advocates and why and how it could benefit them*
5. *Preparing the communications department to be 'digital ready' and equipped to build a genuine online community around the brand and nurture a positive brand narrative.*

Taken all together, Fusionbrand's hundred-plus recommendations mapped out a way forward for the agency, starting with tackling the smaller and more easily remedied problems and grasping the immediate opportunities, the low-hanging fruit. Many of these tactical actions have now been taken, with very obvious success, and the agency is already working with us to implement the next stages and confront the bigger strategic challenges.

Implementation is an important part of the way Fusionbrand works. I have seen too many examples earlier in my career, in Europe, the Middle East and Asia, of smart, well-planned programmes that have failed to deliver because of the way the plans have been translated into action.

The devil, as ever, is in the detail, and I can remember some gruesome instances of hurried or careless implementation that undermined all the hard work at the research and planning stages.

I vowed, at least twenty years ago, that I would always take responsibility for seeing my projects through to a successful conclusion – partly out of loyalty to my customers, but also because I can't bear to see a good programme go off the rails for lack of real follow-through. It offends my professional pride if something I'm associated with fails to achieve its goals, and that tenacity and determination to deliver success to Asian brands has been essential element in Fusionbrand's development as a leading brand consultancy.

In this case, the transition from planning to implementation has been remarkably seamless. The agency has proved to be a realistic and receptive customer. It has been refreshingly keen to take on board the feedback from our brand audit work, without the defensive reactions that are sometimes seen in Southeast Asian businesses that need to make significant changes.

It is often hard to persuade public sector bodies and family-owned firms, for example, to alter long-established ways of doing things, even when the brand audit shows that change is necessary. But these managers were prepared to sit down with us and take a genuinely objective look at the evidence that had led to our suggestions. As a result, all our many recommendations were accepted and we are moving forward to implement them together in a methodical, progressive programme over an 18-month period.

What is most striking about this project, though, is that all the changes and new activities will be possible within the constraints of current budgets.

The agency may even be able to save money, through spending less on expensive and ineffective advertising and on badly-targeted printed collateral and investing carefully in modern, relevant branding initiatives.

While less money will be spent on buying media space for traditional advertising – and less will be wasted on ill-thought-out campaigns and gestures – the agency will be able to use the new tools of social branding and community building to engage and positively influence a much larger number of customers and potential customers.

It will get, as the American military strategists like to say, more bang for its buck. It will be able to adapt and fine-tune its services to the actual needs of its community, responding in real time as those changing needs make themselves felt and building the kind of human, responsive brand that is the surest guarantee of future success.

'Making one-off sales to a large number of customers does not mean you have created a brand.

The true measure of a viable brand is the number of customers with whom you have built a meaningful relationship. And relationships depend on more than a single transactional contact with the customer'

CHAPTER 11

Don't Get Caught Fighting the Last War

Just over one hundred years ago, the generals settled in to begin the mass slaughter of the Great War. Like elderly generals everywhere, of course, they made the mistake of fighting the last war, rather than the next one, and it was many months before they adapted to the new technologies and tactics that were needed for modern warfare in the Europe of 1914.

Today's marketers – with a few honourable exceptions – are busy making exactly the same type of mistake. They are used to deploying the traditional heavy artillery of mass media advertising, but they've hardly begun to respond to the changes brought about by new technologies.

In 1914, despite the recent invention of machine guns, poison gas, radio, motor vehicles and aeroplanes, the one new technology that changed the face of warfare was something cheap, easy to use and available to all. It was barbed wire that altered all the rules and dictated the shape of the battlefield.

A century later, the change that has altered everything for those wishing to build profitable brands is the advent of the internet and social media. Like barbed wire, this is new technology that is cheap, easy to use and available to all. For the old-school marketing generals who are slow to recognise how much the landscape has been transformed, the change represents a major threat.

The difference is that companies can no longer control their brands and how they are perceived by the public. In the past, the big corporates and government agencies were able to use the power of the mass media to create their brands. Now, to a surprisingly large extent, it is the customers who define the brand and who decide what it stands for. And again, it is a new, affordable technology that has changed the rules of the game. Social media, like barbed wire, is something anyone can afford to deploy. It's what you do with it and how you do it, not the sheer weight of budget you can put behind it, that determines whether you can achieve your objectives.

Even 15 years ago, long before social media had entered the arena, a McKinsey study of the world's car manufacturers had already raised the alarm. Something was already starting to go wrong. Traditional marketing methods were not working like they used to do. The McKinsey report highlighted the fact that advertising expenditure and market share no longer moved in lockstep.

Sometimes, McKinsey's researchers pointed out, increased advertising expenditure was still matched by increased market share. But their research also revealed that other carmakers were upping their advertising spend and then looking on in horror as their market share went in the wrong direction. The spread of results was clearly a clue that old certainties were being swept away.

'What's troubling about the distribution is the relatively large number of companies that lose share whether they spend more or spend less on measured advertising,' the McKinsey analysts concluded.

This was unwelcome news for most marketers and was, in the main, quietly ignored or dismissed as being a phenomenon that might just affect the motor industry. But the writing was already on the wall. The major retailers' growing influence on the pricing, presentation and availability of a wide range of products and the increasing fragmentation of the previously all-powerful mass media were combining to change the game.

The worldwide trend towards media fragmentation has accelerated further since then. In the US, the number of magazines has increased by a factor of five between 1980 and 2013. Just twenty years ago, the major US television networks could deliver 70 per cent of the prime-time audience. Now that figure is down to less than 50 per cent, with many American viewers choosing speciality channels like MTV, CNN, ESPN and MSNBC and many more deserting television altogether in favour of online news and entertainment.

Closer to home, in Singapore, the number of TV channels has grown from a mere handful to more than a hundred in the last twenty years – and that doesn't include channels broadcast from Malaysia and Indonesia. In Malaysia itself, there are now more than 200 TV stations, up from three in 1985. Just reaching audiences has become a whole lot more difficult.

If you are still determined to achieve 'share of voice' as one of your marketing goals, and you have the money to do it, it is quite possible to stitch together a media plan that will reach a large proportion of the population. The main TV networks, in Malaysia, Singapore, the US and most other markets, are still 'the tallest midget in the room'. But something more fundamental has changed, something that is not reflected in the traditional marketing metrics of the last few decades.

One-way communication is no longer enough to build a brand. Or, to put it another way, our understanding of what building a brand really means has suddenly become a lot more sophisticated.

In the old mass media economy, with its emphasis on customer acquisition, building a brand was equated with expanding your market share. What has now become clear is that simply knowing that large numbers of people have heard your message a few times and are dimly aware of your product's existence is not enough.

Even making one-off sales of your product to a large number of customers does not mean you have created a brand.

These days, the true measure of a viable brand is generally the number of customers with whom you have built a meaningful relationship. And relationships depend on more than a single transactional contact with the customer.

Until a few years ago, the only way to build continuing two-way relationships with customers was to meet them face to face. For B2B businesses, this meant regular sales and support visits or meetings at conferences and trade shows.

For businesses that were selling to consumers, often through intermediaries such as dealers or retailers, there was no realistic chance of making face-to-face contact with more than a tiny proportion of the customer base. Advertising could carry messages out to the market, but however much you encouraged consumers to get in touch, the only time a two-way conversation took place was when the customer was motivated to complain because something was wrong – hardly the best starting place from which to build a positive relationship.

This lack of a feedback channel was so obvious that some service companies secretly welcomed minor glitches that could be put right quickly, as that gave them an excuse to call customers and apologise, offering them a rare chance to show a human face – or at least, voice.

Research proved, in the UK telecoms market, for example, that the combination of a quick fix and a friendly, apologetic and helpful follow-up call actually increased customer loyalty. People were ready to forgive the telephone company for the occasional breakdown that left them without a phone for a few hours, as long as it was seen to move fast to put things right and took the trouble to say sorry afterwards.

Given these findings, there was certainly a temptation to stage incidents or service breaks simply to create opportunities to talk to customers. I remember one strictly off-the-record meeting in London where it was actually suggested that this might be the way to improve one telecom company's poor reputation for customer service.

'No-one would ever know, and it would do us the world of good,' the marketing director suggested, only half joking.

'Yeah. It would be great for you, but our people would get the blame for the original fault,' said the chief engineer. 'I'm not risking my reputation just to help you boost your customer satisfaction figures.'

Although everyone in the room knew they shouldn't even allow such thoughts to cross their minds, there can't have been anyone who didn't privately wish that some enthusiastic digger driver would plough through a main cable somewhere and give them the excuse to make these calls out to the customers.

These days, Facebook, Twitter, Snapchat and a host of other social media channels provide real opportunities to hold these personalised, one-to-one conversations with customers. Recent figures show that 79% of Malaysia's smartphone owners now use them for social media. And, of course, social media interactions are voluntary, without the negative, intrusive impact of outbound telemarketing campaigns. People who would rush to put the phone down on a cold call are quite willing to become involved in two-way conversations with their telephone company or any other supplier that takes the trouble to engage their interest or talk to them about things that really matter in their world.

As a result, social media content that entertains, informs or amuses the online community is today's key to building the thousands of two-way relationships that add up to a viable brand. In the chapters that follow, we will look at how to make the most of the opportunities it offers to turn the tables on competitors who don't see how the world has changed and are busy fighting the last war, using the outdated weapons they grew up with.

Getting to Grips
with Social Media

'The surviving belief in the controlling power of the ad campaign is certainly one reason why investment in traditional media advertising continues to expand across much of Asia.

After all, a hundred thousand lemmings can't be wrong, can they?'

CHAPTER 12

The Social Media Genie's Out of the Bottle

Culturally, Asian business has a problem with criticism. The notion of constructive criticism is seen as suspect, just as the UK Parliament's concept of 'Her Majesty's Loyal Opposition' would seem incomprehensible to most of our ruling politicians.

The idea that organisations can learn from criticism – both from friends and enemies – is not widely supported in cultures where power has always tended to be concentrated in hierarchical structures with autocratic individuals at the top.

So while the arrival of social media has been welcomed with open arms by the man in the street and the kids on the bus, it has been viewed with horror in the boardrooms of both listed companies and smaller firms.

Asian bosses like to call the tune. And, until very recently indeed, it was absolutely understood that big-budget advertising campaigns gave them that power. Buying large-scale advertising space gave the big boys the ability to pump their messages out, every hour of the day, to a relatively accepting public. It also, less benignly, gave the people who waved these big chequebooks a lot of opportunity to influence the editorial content of the media they used. It gave them a large measure of control over what was seen or heard about themselves, their companies and their products.

The ability to control the discourse is not so clear-cut now. But the surviving belief in the controlling power of the ad campaign is certainly one reason why investment in traditional media advertising continues to expand across much of Asia. After all, a hundred thousand lemmings can't be wrong, can they?

The reality is that this increasing investment in traditional media continues because Asian firms are comfortable with the monologue. They like to create corporate messages that *they are happy with* and then push those messages out to a large audience of consumers – who are assumed to be passive and uncritical recipients.

I glimpsed the underlying attitudes for myself recently, after I had given my talk at a global tourism cities conference in Kuala Lumpur. I was chatting to a group of PR professionals in government and industry when a senior communications man from a government ministry got the ball the rolling.

'The problem I have,' he said, 'is that my Minister and Director General don't like to see any negative comments, complaints or anything bad in the public domain.'

He'd obviously struck a chord. And it didn't only resonate with the public sector staff. The corporate communications director from a listed company recognised the problem immediately and jumped straight in.

'It's the same with my CEO,' he said. 'He's always reminding me that it's my job to keep bad news out of the public domain. We're supposed to stop people complaining on our Facebook page when there is an issue with our service.'

I'm not saying this kind of head-in-the-sand attitude is peculiar to this part of the world. I know it can be found in America and Europe, too. But there are certainly far too many chief executives in Asia who are still wallowing in a sea of self-denial, in a quaint, old-fashioned world where bad news doesn't exist, all their customers are happy and everything is fine and dandy. And a lot of them are about to get a rude awakening over the next year or two.

The other member of our little group at the conference had a classic tale to tell.

'That's just it,' she said. 'When I suggested we set up Facebook, Twitter and YouTube accounts, I had to start off by explaining to my CEO and the directors how they all worked. I told them Facebook would be particularly good for us, as it would give us the chance to be seen as an open and transparent organisation with the interests of our customers at heart.'

'Oh, no,' said the first man. 'I think I know what's coming next.'

'That's right,' she continued. 'They all just stared at me in silence. Then the CEO said "Just to confirm, Sheila. You want us to join Facebook and then let people out there write whatever they want on our Facebook page?"

'I nodded, and he went on. "So if someone – and they don't even have to be a customer – wants to say bad things about us, they can write about us on our Facebook page? And everyone – our competitors, the chairman, the Prime Minister and everyone else – can see it? And this is what you're suggesting we do?"

'I got a rant about how stupid I was, and how it was a ridiculous idea, and that was the end of the discussion. We're still not on Facebook.'

In fact, of course, Sheila's boss had reacted fairly mildly. After all, she still had a job. But this CEO was simply voicing the instinctive opinion of many in Malaysia and neighbouring countries.

Many Asian CEOs are out-and-out control freaks. The idea of letting go of the reins and interacting with customers and consumers as if they mattered seems like a threat to their control of the situation. But they are too late. The horse has bolted. The genie is out of the bottle. Social media exists because people like communicating – and they will do it now, whether you want them to or not. The control the CEO sees as threatened is no longer real. It is just an illusion of control.

Clinging on to control in the face of changes in society is understandable, if you can manage it. Clinging on to an illusion of control is just folly.

In SE Asia, our consumers have leapt ahead of our business leaders. If you want proof of that, compare the computing and communications technology people have in their homes and pockets with what is available in the office. I know big organisations that went into a panic when Microsoft announced it would stop supporting Windows XP in April 2014. If you know anyone who's still using XP at home, I bet it's an old age pensioner.

The idea that Asian business is indulging in serious foot-dragging in relation to social media doesn't just rely on anecdotal evidence. There was an interesting report recently by global public relations firm Weber Shandwick, specifically looking at the use of social media by Asian firms. It didn't mince its words.

'While CEOs in Asia Pacific are engaging [stakeholders] through their company websites, their presence on social networks is non-existent,' it said.

The report was produced by Jon Wade, Weber Shandwick's Head of Digital, Asia Pacific, based in Hong Kong. He's a social media expert and a PR man, so you might suspect a vested interest. But there's proper research behind his conclusions. And he's right.

'Asia-based businesses have been slower than their US and European counterparts to embrace social media, in direct contradiction to the behaviour exhibited by their customers in Asia,' said Wade.

'Traditional business practices still hold sway in Asia,

with executive management teams dominated by older, more conservative board members. We see this changing, but certainly more slowly than is optimal.'

The Weber Shandwick study doesn't go on to report on the prehistoric world of Asian governments. But I can say, from direct experience, that the role of communications in most government institutions has no connection with the world that citizens – sometimes known as voters – inhabit today.

Thinking back to my conversation after the conference speech, what was most striking was the way all of us recognised the same reality.

The fact is that clever, trusted and powerful corporate communications professionals have managed to convince C-level executives and government ministers in Asia that news and events can be managed. They've persuaded them that public opinion can be influenced, critics silenced, crises managed and corporate and personal reputations protected simply by controlling the news and releasing approved corporate information.

But the arrival of social media has burst open their comfortable little world and they are struggling to contain the fallout. The Malaysian government spent nearly £20 million over three years on a UK media and PR company with a brief to build Malaysia's image and polish up its reputation and that of the Prime Minister internationally.

The PR company set to work creating the message that was then pushed out across traditional media. Unfortunately, though, it didn't declare who its masters were and British regulators began to investigate the PR men for producing supposedly independent content on Malaysia without revealing that the country's government was the client.

Instead of successfully raising the profile and reputation of the country and its Prime Minister, the PR company went into liquidation and the Malaysian government was left red-faced after an influential NGO blog got hold of the facts. The NGO didn't tell the story using traditional TV, radio or print media, though. It told the story on its blog and the sorry tale spread across the world at the kind of speed that makes any thought of 'control' obsolete.

When the Malaysian state of Selangor's water supplier, Syabas, shut down four treatment plants and cut off the water to nearly a million homes and businesses, following a diesel spillage on the Selangor River in 2013, it gave a fine demonstration of how *not* to handle a crisis.

People whose taps ran dry naturally turned to the company's website, but found no help or reassurance there – just a press release that told them there was no water in their area. They'd already noticed that. Those who dialled the 1800 number on the home page encountered a recorded message that simply redirected them back to the website.

'I found the Syabas Twitter feed and fired off some tweets asking for more specific information that would allow me to plan for my family of seven, who could not shower, flush their toilets or wash their clothes,' one Selangor resident told me afterwards. 'At first, I didn't blame Syabas. After all, accidents will happen.'

What he'd failed to notice was that Syabas was not listening. To anyone. The company had over 10,000 Twitter followers, but didn't follow one person. Needless to say, there was no response to his tweets. So he tried Facebook.

'I should have known Facebook wouldn't be the answer,' he said. 'They were only reposting the press releases posted on the website. They'd had such a torrent of abuse that they'd disabled the comments function. So I could follow them but I couldn't make any comments or ask for information.'

Syabas actually had a presence on every important social media platform. But it was trying to use social media to broadcast the messages it wanted consumers to hear, rather than to engage with consumers. And that was not just a missed opportunity. It was an outright provocation to worried customers with no working toilets.

One of the main reasons for being on Twitter and Facebook is to be able to spot conversations and trends about your business, your brand and your services. By listening and responding fast in an emergency, a big organisation gets a chance to show its human side. Syabas had that chance and made a total mess of it.

It could have faced up to the situation and addressed the issues in a transparent, prompt and empathetic manner. It could have joined in the conversation, offered sympathy and advice and subtly encouraged positive comment and discussion, building engagement with its public. Instead, it seemed to be doing its best to infuriate waterless customers even more by making them run round in circles following a trail of unhelpful press releases. Yet the whole point of these social media platforms is to allow consumers to interact with the brand and raise the issues that matter to them.

What's sad about this situation is that Syabas actually dealt with the physical problem very efficiently. The engineering worked well and water was restored to more than 650,000 consumers within 36 hours. It should have been a PR success that strengthened the Syabas brand. Instead, it turned into a PR nightmare as hundreds of consumers turned to forums, online newspapers and other social media to vent their anger.

Syabas was used to thinking it could control the message and communicate only what it wanted to be heard. When it lost control, it panicked and froze in its tracks. The result was a badly tarnished reputation and a long hard road back to confidence in the brand.

The point that Syabas and other large organisations must take on board is that the internet has changed their world for ever. Consumers and citizens across Southeast Asia don't look to the corporate spin doctors, the TV commercials, the glossy print ads or billboards for their product and service information any more. Today they have many more sources of news and information and they are increasingly sceptical about anything that comes to them from official sources – or from anyone whose view is clearly driven by a wish to make money out of them.

So they often cobble together several strands of information from disparate sources to form their own opinions, making up their own minds as they go along about which of these sources are likely to be accurate and unbiased and which are driven by vested interests.

And that makes life potentially uncomfortable for all the CEOs, government ministers, public or corporate affairs officers, communications directors and others charged with managing brand communications for companies and other organisations. The well-ordered world they used to know has been replaced by a dynamic, fluid, complicated and chaotic ecosystem where the consumer and the citizen – not the government or the company – define the brand.

Even beginning to come to terms with this brave new world requires an understanding of consumers' decision-making processes, behavioural and emotional science, influencer identification and engagement techniques and, of course, social media platforms and how to use them.

Branding used to be about finding a space in the consumer's mind and positioning your product there.

Today, though, branding demands that firms and governments engage with the consumer's heart – and do it in a genuine, human, transparent way, which is an altogether different and more difficult challenge.

Asian firms and governments find this particularly hard to understand and incorporate into their operations, because it means they can no longer preach and dictate to consumers and citizens and expect them to believe all they're told. They must dare to relinquish control of the message and accept the fact that they may be challenged by increasingly knowledgeable consumers.

The evidence that is all around us shows they are generally nowhere near that point yet. Some have recognised they have a problem, and that's a first step. But many have adopted the ostrich position and have their heads as firmly stuck in the sand as ever.

A few Asian CEOs are stepping out and showing the way forward. These leaders know they must become more accessible and are choosing to develop a role for themselves as spokesperson-in-chief. By creating, contributing to or getting involved in discussions about content originating from staff, customers, potential customers, suppliers and others, on social media and elsewhere, they are showing a willingness to listen and earning the right to claim they are in touch with the reality of their brands' reputations.

One shining instance of this kind of leadership was the response of Air Asia's CEO, Tony Fernandes, when one of his planes crashed off the coast of Kalimantan on a flight from Surabaya to Singapore in December 2014, killing 162 passengers and crew members. I have not always been a fan of Fernandes and his business methods, but his immediate reaction to the tragedy was surefooted and admirable. He spent days at the airport where relatives of the crash victims had gathered, apologising and taking responsibility for the disaster, talking to the families and even staying with them and sleeping on a bench in the arrivals area as they waited in vain for news of their loved ones.

Fernandes was not just being the spokesperson-in-chief for his company. He was embodying its personality and its brand – talking, listening, sympathising and genuinely building a human relationship with the individuals and families involved. It was an extreme example, and the surrounding circumstances were terrible, but this was a superb and meaningful demonstration of how leaders should be ready to get involved and take charge in times of crisis. It was also closely in line with the open, accessible approach Tony Fernandes has brought to other situations that were less tragic and highly charged, in the course of building one of Asia's most successful airlines.

In Europe and the US, this kind of responsiveness is recognised as good management practice. In Asia, it still has an air of dangerous novelty about it. But the effort and investment that organisations put in to be more human and build better two-way communications with consumers, communities and stakeholders is never wasted. Asian companies that want to do business in Europe and America or work together in their home markets with firms from the West will find that this kind of attention to detail is something their overseas partners will demand as a matter of course.

'Word of mouth is always a double-edged sword. You can't afford to make mistakes.

But if you can do it right – with truth, humour, expertise, humanity, generosity and authenticity – nurturing and promoting word of mouth can be a key element in the development and success of your brand'

CHAPTER 13

The Words That Count

How does really successful branding make its presence felt, other than through the long term benefit of increasing sales of a product or service?

What is it that signals, long before the sales figures start to climb, that a brand has achieved the kind of trust, respect, and acceptance that will guarantee success?

The answer – as clever marketers have recognised for many years – is word of mouth.

If customers and members of the broader public are talking positively about a brand, spontaneously mentioning it to their friends and contacts and recommending it to those who are facing buying decisions, sales will follow.

There is a wealth of research, including a massive international study carried out by Nielsen, that proves the importance of word of mouth. The Nielsen survey, which assessed the views of 28,000 online respondents in 56 countries, found that 92 per cent of consumers trusted 'earned media' – word of mouth and recommendations from friends and family – above all other forms of advertising and publicity.

That's not surprising, I suppose. 'Earned' or 'unbought' recommendations have always been the ultimate prize for marketers, simply because they are so elusive and powerful.

What is interesting, though, is the fact that the 92 per cent trust figure reported by Nielsen was 18 percentage points higher than the equivalent figure reported in its previous survey, just five years earlier. That's a huge jump, and it had occurred at a time when global TV advertising budgets had been increasing at roughly 10 per cent per annum.

Word of mouth is becoming even more important, year by year.

Advertisers have been spending more and more to push their messages out and thrust their brands in front of the general public. But the general public has reacted perversely, placing more and more faith in the messages it gets from people, rather than corporations. In fact, the Nielsen survey showed that people's trust in paid television and newspaper ads had declined by around a quarter in just three years.

But as marketers come to recognise that word of mouth is playing an increasingly important role in deciding the destiny of brands, they need to know exactly what they are talking about.

They need to understand the crucial differences between actual word-of-mouth recommendations – passed on in face-to-face dealings with friends, colleagues and contacts – and online word of mouth, which is typically shared with a wider group of less intimate acquaintances. It is still true that only ten per cent of conversations about products, services and brands occur online. The other 90 per cent take place in the home, at work or in various social settings. But it is not just a matter of *where* things are said. *What* people say is different, depending on whether they are talking in the physical world or communicating via social media.

I had been aware for some years that this was an area where many practitioners – including those who positioned themselves as social media experts – were bluffing, or, to put it more kindly, flying by the seat of their pants. There seemed to be very little useful research into the phenomenon of word of mouth. The academics had largely ignored the subject, while those with an axe to grind or a service to sell were hell-bent on hyping up the significance of online buzz and making great play with the few examples they could find of word-of-mouth campaigns going viral and creating overnight sensations.

So I was very pleased to discover a big, ambitious paper called 'On Brands and Word of Mouth', which was published in the *Journal of Marketing Research* in August 2013. This is probably the largest study yet into how and why people talk about brands, online and offline, and the significant differences between the two. It looked at 600 of the best-known American brands, across 16 different product categories, and analysed the brand characteristics that had emerged as prompting people to talk about them over a four-year period from 2007 to 2010.

Right from the start, this research seemed to be filling in vital gaps in our knowledge about online and offline WOM.

'Word of mouth is not channel neutral,' it said, in that particularly poetic way academics have of breaking interesting and exciting news. 'One cannot automatically generalise the results from online to offline.'

I'd stared at these dry, unemotional statements for several seconds before I realised what they were saying. The key finding was that online and offline WOM are more different than most of us recognise, not least because the motives for the communication are radically different.

According to the research, consumers choose to spread the word about brands for three main sets of reasons – *functional*, *social* and *emotional*.

The *functional* element is all about the straightforward desire to provide information.

The *social* is explained as 'the motive to send social signals to the environment (such as expressing uniqueness, self-enhancement, and a desire to socialise or belong)'.

The third motivation, the *emotional*, is described by the

research team as the wish 'to share positive or negative feelings about brands in order to express these emotions or balance emotional arousal'.

That last category could be anything from wanting to get a gripe off your chest to wanting to share your delight in something that had really got you excited or lifted your spirits.

The research found that the order of importance of these three categories varied enormously between online and offline conversations.

The main drivers of online word of mouth turned out to be social, functional and emotional, in that order.

Offline, however, the order of importance of these motives is exactly the opposite – emotional first, then functional and lastly social.

'Offline conversations, which are mostly in one-on-one settings, are more personal and intimate by nature and thus allow people to share emotions such as excitement and satisfaction,' says the report. 'Online WOM, which usually involves "broadcasting" to many people (eg Twitter), is more appropriate for social signalling (eg uniqueness).'

This has serious implications for marketers. It means, for example, that an online strategy built around social media will work best if it offers something new – either a new product or an intriguing new message – that gives people the chance to earn 'social currency' by sharing or that helps them with other desirable social signalling.

'Social currency', incidentally, is simply the researchers' phrase for kudos, or even what the rest of us might call 'brownie points'.

The early adopters who rush online to talk to the world about new smartphone apps, music tracks or travel bargains are often motivated by the wish to show that they are, if not unique, unusually sharp and well-informed observers, leaders rather than followers, opinion formers rather than sheep.

They share information with friends and followers partly for the pleasure of bolstering this image and partly for the sense of belonging that comes from starting and continuing online discussions.

So a social media strategy that engages and maybe flatters these social signallers has a good chance of success, especially in the brand categories that particularly attract online word of mouth.

The research showed that two thirds of all online conversation falls into just three subject areas – media/entertainment, cars and consumer technology. People who share news and views in these areas can often build large communities of friends and followers, earning the social currency that motivates them and effectively establishing themselves as pundits or commentators in their chosen fields. If you can get them involved as willing recruits and unpaid recommenders for your products, you have a strong basis for social media brand building.

The situation with offline, or 'real', word of mouth is very different. Here the emotional motive is the strongest driver. People are talking to individuals and small groups of friends and contacts, face to face and in real time, and anything that is recognised as social signalling is frowned upon. The subject matter tends to be different, too, with food and drink discussions leading the topic count, way ahead of the inevitable technology, cars and entertainment.

There is still potential for the marketer to encourage and benefit from word of mouth, but a very different approach is required.

If your aim is to tap into the emotions that come with strong brand satisfaction or the excitement people feel about a purchase they have just made, you need to help them share these emotions offline. And the key to this is the existence of stories they can pass on to their friends.

A customer whose delivery driver came back three times to make sure his parcel went to the right person has a positive tale to tell. The car buyer who's just discovered his new vehicle really does deliver 15 kilometres per litre will be keen to talk about it. The passenger who was quickly and cheerfully upgraded as compensation after the airline had mishandled her booking has a story to share that friends will be interested to hear.

These are all good examples of the way branding goes far beyond the marketing department. It's the responsive, customer-friendly performance of the delivery driver and the airline reservation staff that creates these positive stories and wins the goodwill and word of mouth, not the ingenuity of some wild-eyed genius in an ad agency. It's the design and production quality of the new car that makes it capable of 15km to the litre and puts flesh on the bones of the brand promises. In all these cases, the offline WOM is a spontaneous response to brand values that can be seen to be working. The reality creates the stories and the stories cry out to be told.

A lot of offline word of mouth is like this. You can create the preconditions for WOM to occur, but you can't make it happen. You can lead a horse to water, but you can't make it drink. You can hope customers will tell others about their great experiences with your product and your people, but you can't bribe, cajole or force them.

On the other hand, this is one area where old-fashioned mass media advertising approaches can be relevant, and where a link may exist between online and offline WOM.

In the old days, the ad agency's goal was often to come up with a TV commercial that would be so funny, so dramatic, so unusual or even just so silly that people would be talking about it at work and with their friends the next day. Sometimes a celebrity would endorse the product. Sometimes the copywriters would come up with a line that would escape to become part of the language ('I'm lovin' it', 'It's the real thing', 'Where's the beef?' or 'Just do it').

That can still happen with heavyweight mass market television campaigns, but how many firms can afford those? The good news is that it can also happen now as a result of much smaller, more affordable online initiatives that are based on customers' real-world experiences. An idea that has the potential to take on a life of its own like this will only need a small push to set it in motion. If it truly has legs, it will be picked up, shared and forwarded online, becoming the subject of digital WOM as the social signallers pass it around.

It will then, ideally, broaden out into the world of offline WOM, with people telling their friends about it, not to earn social currency but to share the emotional pleasure of a feelgood experience.

In truth, this is an ideal situation and it will not occur often. And though you can encourage it, you can't *make* it happen. If it does, you must be ready for it, share it and enjoy it, but not be lured into thinking that you can do it again to order. It is always unlikely that you are the one marketer in the world who has stumbled upon the Holy Grail. It's much more likely that you have struck lucky once, through doing the right sort of things, and that it won't happen to you again for some months or years, if ever.

So the important lesson from the *Journal of Marketing Research* study of brands and word of mouth is that online and offline WOM don't usually cross over, and that they need to be seen and approached in different ways – though it's also true that what you do offline goes a long way towards determining your reputation online. Since the online space offers access to large numbers of potential customers and people's desire for social signalling can be a powerful asset in your brand-building, this is the obvious place to concentrate your resources.

But just because social media make it easier than ever to connect with people, we should not think the job is done.

In fact, of course, social media make it easier than ever before to take the first steps in connecting with people. But they are only first steps. The real connection only starts to grow after that first link has been made, as you begin to build trust. That comes from demonstrating your expertise, your helpfulness and, most important of all, your authenticity. If people who come across you online see everything you put out as self-serving, grasping, sales-oriented and only concerned with taking, rather than giving, the only online WOM that will result will be negative.

And that is a whole lot worse than no word of mouth at all. There's a famous line that's always, and wrongly, attributed to the American writer Mark Twain. It says: 'A lie can go halfway round the world while the truth is still pulling its boots on.'

Whoever said it or didn't say it, there's a lot of truth in that. Lies spread fast and cause a lot of damage, and even true but negative comments seem to share that particular ability to outrun any kind of good news. Word of mouth is always a double-edged sword. If you're going to do it, make sure you do it right. If you are setting out with the conscious intention of encouraging WOM and making it work for you, you can't afford to make mistakes.

But if you can do it right – with truth, humour, expertise, humanity, generosity and authenticity – nurturing and promoting word of mouth will be a key element in the development and success of your brand.

'Samsung spent an eye-watering US$14bn on marketing in 2014 – roughly the GDP of countries like Cambodia and Laos.

That can't go on. It is quite possible that this is the moment of Peak Advertising, the watershed point in business history where even those global giants with the deepest pockets have to start thinking again'

CHAPTER 14

The Red-Hot Brand That Just Won't Advertise

Answer quickly: Who's the third largest smartphone manufacturer in the world?

You know the top two – Samsung and Apple, obviously.

But how much do you know about Xiaomi?

According to technology research giants IDC, Xiaomi has shot from way down the table to Number 3, ending 2014 with a global market share of 5.2 per cent. That's nearly half the size of Apple in this market, and a quarter the size of Samsung. It's bigger than Lenovo, LG and Huawei, and far ahead of Sony, Nokia and all the rest.

Outside Asia, hardly anyone has heard of Xiaomi. Even in Asia, it's not a name you see screaming at you from billboards, plastered over the sides of buildings or beamed out at you from your television. Yet this extraordinary Chinese company has climbed, from a standing start with the release of its first product in August 2011, to capture sales of nearly 70 million smartphones a year. In the first half of 2015, it sold twice as many phones as it did a year earlier. It's a staggering performance, to build such a huge brand in so little time, and Xiaomi has done it the modern way, with virtually no advertising at all.

Xiaomi doesn't advertise, because it doesn't need to.

When its new models are released, the online buzz is so

strong that they sell out immediately. The company has no retail stores, no distributors and no sales force, as all its products are sold online, through its own website and Facebook pages. And the business model works.

The Singapore launch of the Redmi Note phablet in mid-2014 saw the entire stock sold out in just eight seconds. In Malaysia, where the Redmi 1S model was launched in September 2014, there was no such rush – it took nearly six minutes for Xiaomi's fans to snap up every available smartphone. In Indonesia, 50,000 1S phones were pre-ordered in the first week, while in India, in December 2014, 50,000 Notes were bought on the first day.

This is the pay-off from getting every aspect of the branding just right, including engaging consumers and generating interest through social media.

Xiaomi's founder, Lei Jun, is a Steve Jobs fan – some might even say a Steve Jobs clone – and he has set the tone for his company with a customer-focused mission statement that says: 'We are passionate about being the most user-centric mobile internet company, creating innovation that everyone can enjoy.'

But good intentions are not the whole story. Xiaomi produces capable products, with great build quality and technology that is often on a par with Samsung and Apple's best, at aggressively low prices – less than half what the market leaders are charging. It even offers some features, such as scratch-proof gorilla glass screens, extended-life batteries and the ability to customise the software according to user preferences, that seem more advanced than its rivals. Accessories such as cases and power banks are ridiculously cheap and customer service is fast, efficient and, above all, human. Xiaomi's launch day flash sales are major online events and some opportunists who are lucky enough to secure first-day purchases go straight onto eBay to sell them on at a profit.

The company places a few inexpensive teaser ads on Facebook, but its total advertising spend is minimal. Most of the excitement is generated through Xiaomi's deft use of its own Facebook pages, which have 720,000 likes and feed fans a well-judged stream of announcements, special offers, tech news and human interest stories that just keeps people coming back. Its main Twitter feed is lively and quirky and has 132,000 followers, and Xiaomi also runs Twitter accounts in many languages, including Bahasa accounts for both Malaysia and Indonesia. The company's customers do most of the promotional work for free, as word-of-mouth enthusiasm spreads across the internet and friends, bloggers and online journalists tip each other off about the next flash sale.

Xiaomi's global head of marketing, Amanda Chen, was named as one of AdAge's Women to Watch for 2015. She sees the involvement of fans and social media conversations as defining a large part of her company's unique appeal. When asked about how Xiaomi would counter a huge Google ad campaign for its Android One launch in India, Chen pointed out that it could respond in kind, but that it deliberately chose not to.

'By hiring an ad agency or outsourcing to a huge production house, everything would look good. And we do have the cash,' she said.

'But it would be a different company. Because if there are no fans involved, they wouldn't be feeling like they are part of the event.'

The contrast between Xiaomi and the market leader, Samsung, is striking.

Samsung spent an eye-watering US$14 billion on marketing in 2014 – roughly the GDP of some smaller countries like Cambodia and Laos.

That can't go on. Even with Samsung Electronics revenues running at around US$220 billion (equal to the

GDP of Portugal), it is just not possible to sustain that level of marketing spend. Not for Samsung – not for anyone.

It is quite possible that this is the moment of Peak Advertising, the watershed point in business history where even those global giants with the biggest sales and deepest pockets have to start thinking again.

Despite the deluge of advertising in every country and every possible media channel, Samsung's smartphone sales have fallen. In June 2015, the company reported disappointing quarterly profits for the seventh time in a row, triggered by a 20% drop in smartphone sales. I doubt if the Korean giant's managers are seriously worried yet about Xiaomi's growth, but they should be.

Samsung can keep throwing money at the problem – and if it throws enough, it may be able to prop up high levels of sales for years to come. But the rate of return on these huge investments in marketing will inevitably continue to shrink.

Ultimately, a 20th-century-style company like Samsung will have to change or die in the face of competition from a lean, stripped-down and ambitious rival that can survive and profit without the need for this kind of spending. Xiaomi has the winning combination of a powerful, attractive brand, cheap and desirable products and an infinitely scalable online sales model, and its momentum is beginning to look unstoppable. Having made a huge impact throughout Asia, it is now turning a hungry eye on other promising markets such as Brazil.

What's even worse news, for Samsung and for the advertising-driven multinational giants in many other industries and markets, is the fact that people have noticed this shift beginning to occur. More and more companies are starting to see that there is the opportunity to use social media and other modern tools and techniques to build businesses and brands that can compete without having to match the big boys' spending.

Even three or four years ago, I would not have dared to call my book *Stop Advertising, Start Branding*. Here at Fusionbrand, we were already beginning to get a sense of what could be achieved on smaller budgets, but the range of online tools was still too narrow to form the base for a major branding initiative.

Now we have those tools, and we have the examples, like Xiaomi, that prove it can be done with spectacular success – and not just in affluent Western countries, but in the less mature markets of Southeast Asia as well.

It's not easy. Competing with established and well-funded multinationals never is. But companies that know what they want to do and know how to make full use of the resources available in today's online world can make it happen. At the same time, as I have stressed elsewhere, tapping into the power of social media and customer-generated content will not work, in the long term, if companies don't also go back to basics. They must make sure their technologies, products, processes, data collection and use, staff capabilities and customer service provision are all up to scratch and capable of supporting the brand and embodying its values.

Few companies can assess their own performance in these areas accurately and without bias – the view from inside is always distorted by wishful thinking. But there are now several specialised branding consultancies in Southeast Asia (led, of course, by Fusionbrand) that can provide a candid outsider's appraisal and make the appropriate recommendations. Rigorous research, comprehensive audits of internal and external branding and careful data collection and analysis can help build up an objective view that will provide a solid basis for planning and action.

In the end, though, the secret of great branding is its inclusivity. A great brand gets the customer on its side. A great brand turns happy customers into advocates and recommenders and turns sceptical consumers into potential buyers. Customers want the brand to thrive and succeed because they gain something valuable from its presence in their lives, whether that's a succession of great products or the smiles and knowledge they get from coming across amusing or interesting comments on Facebook or Twitter.

Smart branding takes account of all these factors. It invests in the relationships it builds, responding and giving something back in a way no mass media ad campaign can ever do. It is not about hype. On the contrary, it is about authenticity and connecting with the real world.

For all Xiaomi's dazzling success and popularity with its customers, one of the characteristics of its brand-building is a refusal to over-promise. Customers who have bought a smartphone via one of its flash sales are naturally excited and keen to get their hands on the new product as soon as possible, but Xiaomi shrewdly manages expectations by quoting a delivery date of about three weeks.

This gives it the opportunity to beat its promised date, which it almost invariably does, since the new smartphone will usually be despatched immediately and be in the customer's hands within five days. That's smart, sensitive thinking, insulating the company from most of the inevitable hiccups that occur in any distribution system and showing its cultural preference for under-promising and over-delivering, for the benefit of its customers.

Xiaomi is still the upstart challenger, but its explosive growth has nothing to do with chance. It has worked hard to create a new business model that threatens to upset the status quo and a brand that guarantees continuing success in this fiercely competitive global market. Unless you have friends who own Redmi smartphones, you may not have heard much about the company yet. But you'll definitely be hearing a lot more about it in the next few years.

'If your customers come up with interesting stories online, share them, like them, respond and comment. Don't just wait for topics relevant to your business. Focus on your customers.

Take the opportunity to show you are interested in them, over and above their potential as buyers of your products'

CHAPTER 15

Social Media's Rule of Thirds

You want to use social media as a serious branding tool. Why wouldn't you, considering its power, its reach, its cost-effectiveness and its ability to help you build relationships and develop your brand?

But if you're serious about it, there is a lot to learn.

Traditional marketers who have been brought up on big-budget advertising campaigns tend to lumber into the social media area without realising quite how different this new world is. They are used to bludgeoning their audiences into submission with repeated television commercials or grabbing their attention with huge billboards on the drive into town. What they are not used to is engaging with people who know what they want and are ready to click away almost instantly if they're not getting it.

Social media must earn the time and attention of its audience. And that means giving, as well as taking. If you manage to give the impression – as so many businesses do – that you're only in it for the money you can extract from the consumer's purse or wallet, you will lose.

So how do you give? What is it that you can do to build a relationship your social media audience will value and want to maintain?

There is a rule of thumb in social media marketing circles that is usually known as The Rule of Thirds.

No-one can quite agree on what the thirds in question are, and any number of different experts and would-be gurus seem to want to lay claim to the Rule of Thirds as their own creation, but there is certainly the germ of an important idea here that you can use to develop a winning social media strategy for your brand.

The Rule of Thirds says this:

- Only one-third of your social media content should be promotional, selling material. Any more and people will start to switch off. People don't come to social media to be sold to. They'll tolerate – sometimes even enjoy – a light touch, but heavyhandedness is death.
- One-third should be curated content – stuff you've come across that will be interesting or useful to others in and around your industry, or third party material that will be helpful in some way to your readers. By selflessly sharing this, you are contributing to the wisdom and resources of the social media community and, in a sense, earning the right to be listened to.
- One-third of your social content should be personal, based on personal interactions and experiences. It should be subtly, cumulatively building your personal brand. That means being sociable, witty, light-hearted, real. It also means being responsive, answering and asking questions, dealing respectfully with criticism, welcoming people in and showing a readiness to go out to meet them and their interests.

There are any number of pithy formulations of the Rule of Thirds. Some people want to dress it up as The Three Cs (Creation, Curation and Conversation) or The Three Ps (Professional, Profitable and Personal), though that last example only works if you understand that 'profitable' here has to mean 'giving some sort of profit or payoff to the reader, not the writer'.

Others give up on trying to package these insights up into a neat little mnemonic and just talk about the need to balance out the three strands of activity. You need to promote, share and converse, they say – and if any one of these is either missing or overdone, you will fall short of achieving the best possible results.

So let's look at the three imperatives one by one.

1. YOUR BUSINESS: Promoting, selling, sharing your own branded content and making sure people are aware of your product and your business is the last thing that's going to be overlooked by any marketer. As hinted at before, though, there is a real danger here of going too far, shouting too loud and selling too hard.

Part of the value of thinking in terms of the Rule of Thirds, however you define it, is that it encourages the idea that reining in your enthusiasm for selling and lead generation is essential to avoid alienating your audience. This third should include content such as company blog postings, details of your webinars and networking events and information about your new products or new ways of using what customers have already bought from you.

2. INDUSTRY TRENDS AND TOPICS: The curating and sharing function is the least obvious aspect of social media marketing activity and is highly likely to be neglected by those who do not have their eye on the ball. Even without going looking for them, you are bound to stumble across interesting, amusing or enlightening articles, videos and blogs that have some relevance to your industry or your customers' enthusiasms and concerns. The moment you share these, you send positive social signals – that you are a likeminded soul, tuned in to what interests people, that you are a giver and not just a taker, and that you are a potential source of useful information in the future. There are several good reasons there for your audience to warm to you and to wish to follow the rest of your content.

If you need to find more interesting material to share, the obvious way is to carry out keyword searches or to follow hashtags that use your industry's terminology or mention place names that might be relevant. Every industry, sector and geography has influencers and thought leaders whose ideas are worth passing on, but one less obvious source of content may be your direct competitors. Sharing content that originates from them makes you look collegiate, objective and confident, positioning you as a well-rounded information source within the industry.

Old-school marketers might yelp that even mentioning your competitors gives them credibility. New-school brand builders retort that anyone who thinks a car buyer is not aware of the existence of Toyota or that a smartphone user doesn't already know about Apple and Samsung is living in a dream world.

There are subtle degrees of sharing, too, that you can take advantage of. You can just pass content on, by straightforward sharing and retweeting. Or you can add your own spin and commentary. Using a social media management tool like HootSuite, for example, you can identify trending topics related to your industry, track keywords and collect a whole range of useful analytics. There are also tricks you can use to encourage people to take notice, such as making sure, when you add your comment to something you are sharing, that you mention the names of people or companies touched on in the shared material.

This namedropping is known as 'share baiting' or 'ego baiting'. It's not subtle, but it doesn't have to be. People are acutely sensitive in this area – most of us could spot our own name on the page of a telephone directory at a distance of 80 yards – and they are much more likely to share or retweet something that talks about them. That's human nature, and part of the art of building brands through deft use of social media is recognising how human nature works and what you can do with it.

3. YOU: This is the third that separates the men from the boys. It's your opportunity to share your positive and negative experiences with brands and establish an online personality that will keep people interested in what you have to say. It's also the part of the online presence that is most often mishandled. People don't want to read about what you had for breakfast, unless you experimented with yak-flavoured lassi or shared your fried eggs or curry puff in an early-morning *tête-à-tête* with the Prime Minister. They want to be surprised, amused or made to think in new ways about familiar topics.

If I respond to a tweet about something serious or funny that's cropped up in the news, or pass on something I've seen in a magazine or found online, it helps build my personality profile. But only if I've judged it right.

I have a particular weakness for airline safety instruction videos – the good, the bad, the ugly, and the deliberately or accidentally hilarious – and I've noticed that there is a sharp uptick in the number of people following me and visiting my blog every time I share one of these video clips.

I'm in the communication business, so the whole question of how ideas are put across is important to me. But I doubt that sharing a video of a rapping flight attendant on Southwest Airlines or Air New Zealand's (swiftly withdrawn) 'babes on the beach' safety instructions epic directly brings me any new business for my company, Fusionbrand. After all, we call ourselves 'Asia's leading customer-driven brand consultancy', rather than 'Asia's leading critics of pre-flight safety videos'.

So it's not my business expertise that's attracting these new contacts. It's the personality and presence that's gradually built up through hundreds of little, apparently irrelevant, contributions to the social community. That's all right. I don't want to be selling to people all the time. But I'd bet that any of these 'purely social' contacts of mine who suddenly needed the advice of a specialist Southeast Asian branding consultancy would be more likely to call me than my competitors.

Another important element of the Rule of Thirds' third and last third is direct or indirect customer input. If your customers come up with interesting stories online, share them, like them, respond and comment. Don't just wait for topics to arise that are immediately relevant to your business. Focus on your customers. Take the opportunity to show you are interested in them, as businesses and as people, over and above their potential as buyers of your products. Congratulate them on their successes, help them solve their problems and take part in the general online conversations they contribute to. The ties that connect people on social media are built up through a web of tiny, Lilliputian threads that gradually draw them closer together.

If you're short of worthwhile content for this third of your social media presence, remember that you don't have to be funny or directly relevant every time you appear online. If you can post links to material that's topical, stimulating or even, in the broadest sense, educational, that will win you friends as well. All you have to do is be interesting and, above all, avoid being boring.

Being boring is the worst of all social media crimes, and there's no excuse for it.

It's an interesting world we live in, and there's always a huge amount of fresh and fascinating free content out there that's just waiting to be shared. A great resource for this is the TED lectures, nearly 2000 short talks on a vast range of important and unexpected topics, from love, magic and psychology to Islamic superheroes and ultra-running. The TED lectures are always wise, witty and well-informed, often quirky and unpredictable, and frequently provocative as well. I have yet to meet anyone who wasn't knocked out by filmmaker Andrew Stanton's brilliant and scurrilous talk on storytelling ('But you f★★k one goat…') or moved by Sir Kenneth Robinson's heartfelt plea for a rethink of the way we educate our children. When in doubt, share a link to a TED lecture and I guarantee it'll help your profile.

Rules are made to be broken. There may be times when you're launching a new product or responding to a product recall crisis and you need to put the Rule of Thirds to one side for a while.

It's only a broad guideline, a general indication of how best to grow and nurture a broad and positive social media presence. But it's firmly based on experience of what works.

Even in this new and fast-evolving social media environment, there is a big difference between the performance of the best and the worst practitioners. Aiming for a balanced online presence, based on splitting your contributions between your business, your industry and your more personal side, is one way to make sure your social media efforts help towards the overall goal of building a rounded, credible, human and respected brand.

'This individual must be ready to take on a key role in the engine room of the business.

The community manager must have the authority to take charge of the brand and chivvy other parts of the organisation into line if they are not pulling their weight'

CHAPTER 16

Make Way for the Community Manager

In Asia, everything happens in coffee shops. That might be a slight exaggeration, but just watch what the local politicians do as soon as election time is near. If they want to win, they make a beeline for the coffee shops and sit there for hours, shooting the breeze with hawkers and fishermen and bankers and shopkeepers and journalists and whoever happens along.

They are talking, swapping stories, making new friends, getting known and spreading their ideas. But it's a two-way process. They are also listening, judging the mood, picking up titbits of information and gossip.

Sometimes they are openly trying to persuade the people they're talking to. More often, and more subtly, they are just becoming part of the conversation – influencing it, perhaps, but not trying to force the issue or take control of the discussion.

These guys are pros. They know what they're doing and they know what works. They know that the comments after they've gone on somewhere else are largely what decide people's attitudes. Of course, people will talk about the politician when his back is turned. They'll talk to their friends and neighbours, their families and business contacts, to people they know and even to other people who just happen to be sitting at the next table.

Some of that chat will be good. Some will be neutral, teasing or undecided. But, as long as it isn't downright negative and destructive, the politician welcomes it all. There's nothing, nothing at all, worse than being ignored.

If you have been struggling to get to grips with the idea of social media's place in business and society, it's probably helpful to think of Facebook, Twitter, Instagram, Snapchat, Tencent Weibo, LinkedIn and all the rest as the social equivalents of a row of *kopi tiams*. You get the same kind of natural, spontaneous, often undirected chatter, punctuated with more serious, sometimes heated, discussions. No-one's in charge and no-one's there out of duty. Everyone's voice gets heard and great wisdom may rub shoulders with extraordinary foolishness.

The big question – in practice – is how businesses can make the most of all this, and what they should be doing to use all this online conversation to build and strengthen their brands.

Like traditional advertising campaigns, this kind of work obviously demands skill and ingenuity. But unlike traditional advertising campaigns, it doesn't call for big budgets. And even if you do have a lot to spend, you can't hope to compete with the big global brands. What you need is bright, responsive people to spot the opportunities, react to them on the fly and represent the online personality and values of your brand.

This is a completely new role, and it requires a new department, quite separate from the traditional marketing or advertising departments. We need a new title for the people who develop and run this department and deploy the specific skills needed to carry out the new role and make a success of it. They are now usually referred to as 'community managers', though this title is still largely unknown to non-specialists. If you have the right person in this role – someone who is quick-thinking, aware and tuned in to what's being said (and how it's being said) within the online community – it can make a huge difference to the organic growth of your brand.

The fact is, like the coffee shop conversations about politics and politicians, online discussions about your industry, your product area and your brand will happen whether you like it or not.

If you turn away from the conversation, you make it inevitable that people will talk about you behind your back. But if you become part of the conversation, you can influence people's thought processes and influence the way the discussion is going.

Naturally, there are limits to what you can do and how you can do it. You cannot get away with trying to bully or browbeat people in social media conversations, and anything that is nakedly self-serving and crudely trying to sell your product will be counterproductive. No-one would want their downtime in the *kopi tiam* hijacked by a politician shouting his wares, and the same applies online.

But if you learn to respect the nuances, understand the psychology involved and develop an empathy with the customers and commenters who take the trouble to communicate online, the payoffs can be remarkable.

Traditional marketers like to talk about the brand story. But if you think in terms of a story, you are generally looking at something that has a beginning, a middle and an end – and that generally has one author. That's not how things are in the social media context. You can't tell your story, control it and expect people to take it at face value. Instead, you have to think in terms of an ongoing narrative, evolving organically and developing out of the voices of many different authors.

No-one should run away with the idea that this is an easy, cheap-and-cheerful alternative to traditional marketing. Nurturing and building the brand in this way calls for someone in the role of community manager who has a real understanding of business and customers and the authority to make brand-critical decisions in real time. It's a senior role – as important as anyone in the company except, perhaps, the CEO – and it's essential to resist the temptation to recruit some bright, enthusiastic youngster who loves technology and knows social networks but does not have real business experience.

You need a senior person who can operate at general manager level, take full responsibility and get it right most of the time. The community manager must work with and report directly to the CEO and should be able to rely on the boss's backing and support through thick and thin.

You will be looking for someone with a sales, marketing, communications or PR background, several years' experience and a solid track record of substantial achievement. And people like that don't come cheap, even in the relatively low-wage economies of Southeast Asia.

In Malaysian terms, recruiting at this level this would imply a salary of maybe 150,000 to 180,000 ringgit a year (US$45,000 to US$50,000). In Jakarta or Bangkok, the figures would probably be similar, though the price tag in Singapore or Hong Kong would naturally be rather higher. You will also need to budget for another RM100,000, maybe a little more, for a couple of support staff.

The point is that this individual must be ready to take on a key role in the engine room of the business. The community manager must have the power to take charge of the brand and chivvy other parts of the organisation into line if they are not pulling their weight. With the CEO's backing and encouragement, the community manager should have the authority to insist that every interaction with customers and the public is in character and in keeping with consumers' needs and the brand's values.

That ought to mean – quite apart from all the work on

developing a social media presence – taking the initiative to monitor and manage every imaginable touchpoint, every single place where the brand and its public meet. It will involve working with sales to ensure front-line staff are trained and motivated to greet customers with warmth, energy and curiosity and a genuine intention to satisfy their need for value. It will mean working with customer service people to make sure queries are answered, complaints are resolved and returns and replacements are handled quickly and positively, with grace and good humour.

Because the community manager is in constant touch with the views and moods of the consumer, through a range of social media channels, he or she becomes the conduit bringing real-time feedback to the rest of the business.

When things are going well, there will always be clues as to what could be done to make the most of the momentum. When something goes wrong – if a new product starts to fail, rumours are spread about the company or unfair press coverage creates a negative impression – it is the community manager who is likely to hear the bad news first.

In this kind of crisis situation, the CEO must be able to rely on the community manager to intervene immediately with well-judged contributions that help, rather than hinder, the company. While the company will already have a crisis plan, there are bound to be unexpected twists and turns to cope with. There may be no time to check the wording or even the content of a social media response, especially if it's all happening at 3 o'clock in the morning, so top management needs to have a lot of faith in the community manager's commercial and political judgment and communication skills.

Not every company can make the adjustment to this new, holistic brand-building approach. Not every company that wants to will be able to find a community manager with all the skills or potential to do the job well. Many will have to think in terms of converting a more traditional marketing or sales specialist to take on the role, possibly with the help of some pretty intensive training in social media techniques and conventions.

Even with the right person in place, there is still a lot of work to do to get the whole business aligned with the new realities. Organisations that are serious about it need to be prepared to invest in their people and processes, decentralise their decision-making and spend substantial amounts of money to create high quality content that will be liked, forwarded, shared and tweeted about across social media. They will need to dedicate time and resources to make sure that both positive comments and complaints are responded to in a human, transparent manner. But they will not need to spend anything like the amounts that have traditionally been poured into mass media ad campaigns, with all the waste and imprecise targeting that these one-way communications brought with them.

I am not saying there is never a case for smaller, focused advertising campaigns, aimed at an identifiable and reachable audience, as part of the overall brand building and marketing effort. But the days are gone when the customers you wanted to reach could be scooped up by a few million dollars' worth of repetitive TV commercials.

If you still have budgets on that scale, there are better – and more accountable – ways to spend them. If you don't, the good news is that we are operating in a changing world where you can make much more modest budgets work just as well. There are plenty of blind alleys and elephant traps along the way, but the opportunity is there for companies big and small to build strong, profitable and resilient brands without spending millions to do it.

'Key activities for the community manager include blogging on the company's web pages and on external sites, coming up with ideas to drive traffic to the brand and building relationships with early adopters, friends, enemies and partners.

It's a big portfolio of responsibilities – and it makes for a long working day'

CHAPTER 17

A Day in the Life

The community manager's task is to reinforce the brand, set the direction of travel through conversations with prospects, pundits and happy and unhappy customers, and identify opportunities to build visibility and engage people through online discussions and communities.

It's a job that involves many responsibilities – for awareness building, sales, retention, customer service, recruitment, marketing and engagement, as well as content creation and brand advocacy. Some firms like to split these responsibilities between a social media department and the community manager, but I always prefer to keep them within the same department, as it leads to more consistent performance.

Key activities for the community manager will include blogging on the company's own web pages and on external sites, coming up with ideas to drive traffic to the brand and building relationships with early adopters, friends, enemies and partners. It's a big portfolio of responsibilities – and it makes for a long working day.

07.30am
Review emails. Check key platforms to identify any urgent issues and flag for attention and discussion in the morning meeting.

Check Twitter and Facebook, probably Pinterest, too, for comments about our new packaging. Respond immediately to all private messages and flag corporate messages for discussion. Scan analytics for any glaring discrepancies.

Snatch breakfast.

09.00am

At the office, review reports from social media tracking tools like Google Analytics, HootSuite, Sprout Social and TrackUr to assess recent activity.

Check Twitter, Facebook and LinkedIn for company-specific posts and other relevant content, especially complaints that need to be addressed personally or flagged for wider discussion.

Check news feeds and the internet for new content that may be worth sharing later or offer opportunities to build on existing narratives.

10.00am

Department meeting to evaluate social media issues flagged earlier, prioritise responses and determine how to handle those that need immediate action.

Review response times, identify any fires that are burning and plan the team's approach to them. If there are complaints or customer comments on negative experiences involved, decide whether it's worth trying to contact the complainer and continue the discussion offline, out of the social media spotlight. When a complaint has been raised in a public forum, though it is always best to respond in the same forum.

Make plans with the team responsible for tracking and engaging influencers about activities and targets for the week.

Discuss topics with blog writers and the editorial team responsible for commissioning articles, co-ordinating projects to develop topical, positive themes linked to current trends.

Map out blog titles for the next period (usually three months ahead). Research any industry issues that could bubble up to become significant and develop broad ideas to address them in fresh and interesting ways.

11.30am

Meet other departments and inform them about the next quarter's editorial plans and any new discussions, comments or complaints that are relevant to them. The community manager and his team provide the social media eyes and ears for these departments. There will be good news and bad news, but it is always important that they are aware of it and ready to make whatever contribution is required to support the brand.

Contact all those – usually customer support, sales and the fulfilment and shipping/transport departments, but sometimes product development or finance, too – who need to take action in response to new discussions, comments and complaints. Review progress reports on earlier issues and close off those that have been dealt with. If necessary, invoke the CEO's support to ensure that remedial action is taken seriously.

12.30pm

Grab lunch, either at the desk or out of the office. If at the office, use the time to catch up on industry and market news and developments in media tracking and analytics, real-time search and lead integration tools.

01.30pm

Review tasks from morning session and track progress of team activities. Check media and academic coverage of trends in social engagement and any other insights that may be beneficial.

02.00pm
Meet sales team members to identify tactical promotions and new developments planned for the near future and work out where they fit in the company's strategic plan for social media activity.

03.00pm
Check Twitter, Facebook and LinkedIn company and personal accounts. Retweet or share relevant posts and take the opportunity to comment on topical issues. Interact with followers and respond to direct messages and general requests.

03.30pm
Meet consumer data team to discuss how data is being collected and processed and what can be done to make this more effective. Agree on new protocols for communicating with customers who have not made a purchase in the last three months.

04.00pm
Quiet time. Develop ideas for future blogs, usually based on emerging stories related to the industry, product innovations or corporate developments.

05.00pm
Prepare review of the team's performance, covering activities and interactions and the latest information on reputation, responses and trends. Compile numbers and charts for social media report that can be shared with the team and – importantly – the CEO, the community management team's key sponsor.

05.30pm
Discuss report with team members and include their input in final version.

06.00pm
Deliver the daily report to CEO's office. If required to discuss the report, wait for CEO to become available. If not, leave. It's been a long day.

Snatch social life.

09.30pm
Check in on Twitter, LinkedIn and Facebook. The long day's not quite over. Respond diplomatically to angry tweet blaming us for faults in product made by our fiercest rivals. Flag potentially controversial issue for discussion in the morning.

Snatch Milo. Bed.

'You have to get stuck in, respond to other people's views and gradually, bit by bit, build an online personality for your brand.

It's not about doing social; it's about being social'

CHAPTER 18

Facebook: You Really Can't Afford to Ignore It

Social media trends may come and go, but Facebook is simply too big, too powerful and too well established to be ignored. As the biggest game in town, by a country mile, it has something to offer every type of organisation, with a whole heap of features and tools that can improve your business. But a lot of companies are rushing into Facebook without any proper planning or understanding. Your community manager and his team will be developing and managing your Facebook page 24/7. To get the most out of it, they will need to know Facebook inside out and be ready to take advantage of new developments and opportunities as they occur.

What is it?

You know what Facebook is. Everybody does. It's an online social network that is like a lot of big rooms, crammed with more than 1.4 billion consumers. Those 1.4 billion consumers are in rooms that they want to be in, doing things they want to do with people they want to be with. While they are there, in those rooms, those consumers are sharing information about where they are, what they are doing, what and who they like, what their interests are and much, much more.

Facebook then takes that mass of information, has a look at it and shares it with similar people across the network. These people then decide if they want to get in touch with each other, become friends and share more information, make comments on what they've read or videos they've seen or join groups of people with similar interests.

The strange thing is, though, that even regular Facebook users, private and commercial, often seem to know very little about the way it works.

For example, when you post a comment on Facebook it has an effective lifespan of about 18 hours. That means it will be active and highly visible for that time, and will then start to sink from view. And what that means, of course, is that you shouldn't generally post more than once a day.

Did you know that? Most of the supposed social media experts I talk to don't. You don't want to be in a situation where your second post is effectively competing with your first and pushing it down the Facebook news feed.

Historically, it was the search engines – Google, Bing and Yahoo – that drove traffic to business sites. Now, Facebook holds the top spot globally for referral traffic to business and other websites, with more than 30 per cent of all referrals. It has an awe-inspiring database of information that can be mined so methodically and accurately that you can market your products very selectively to just those people you want to sell to, at a cost of just a few dollars a day.

When a Facebook user 'likes' your company page, that visitor's Facebook friends see future posts from your company on their own pages. So the more likes you get, the more people see your content. It's like a huge, worldwide pyramid selling scheme on steroids – and it's all completely legitimate and above board.

Facebook's commercial offerings are constantly evolving, so you need to stay abreast of developments. Currently, you can buy ads that appear on the Facebook pages of targeted individuals who have shown an interest in something related to your industry or service and you can also boost content you post on Facebook and choose who it goes to and how much you want to spend.

Facebook has been alert to the potential of the millions of small firms around the world that need cost-effective ways of reaching customers and selling what they produce. It has now developed small business advertising products that allow these low-budget marketers to promote a post on other Facebook pages for as little as US$10 or the local equivalent. Used shrewdly, this can provide interesting, relevant information that readers will welcome and respond to, making brand building much more scientific and targeted than was ever possible with traditional media.

One of the most recent developments, in August 2015, is a new service that gives advertisers the option to buy video ad space on newsfeeds. We have yet to see how popular this will be, but I can see it taking a lot of ad spend away from traditional TV advertising.

Who uses it?

The number of people on Facebook is mind-boggling – well over a billion active users around the world. It is also used by 40 million small businesses, and it is constantly striving to put the 40 million in touch with the billion. These are phenomenal figures, and they simply can't be ignored by any Asian firm or institution that wants to build its brand.

Consumers in all the countries of Southeast Asia have been turning away from traditional news and entertainment sources and engaging with social media. As the biggest game in town, Facebook has been the main beneficiary of this trend, and it has been doing particularly well in Indonesia, the most populous and geographically fragmented country in the region.

Indonesia has 250 million people, more than anywhere else except China, India and the US. But this huge population is spread out over nearly two million square kilometres of often hostile terrain, with 18,000 islands. For TV channels that try to reflect local interests and concerns, and newspapers that depend on physical distribution systems, this fragmented audience has always been extraordinarily hard to reach.

In the past, trying to build brands in Indonesia was nothing short of a logistical nightmare. Access to many parts of the archipelago was difficult and unreliable, making distribution a real challenge. Product often went missing, lost in transit or hijacked by local warlords. It was hardly worth the effort and investment needed to build brands, anyway, when most of the population in the rural areas was so poor that there wasn't much profit to be had from trying to conquer these markets.

Those that did take on the challenge had to find their own ways of doing it. Coca-Cola was one brand that pulled it off, but that was a success built on a unique strategy. Instead of spending on massive advertising campaigns, Coca-Cola focused on the supply chain, showing a grim determination to push the product out into the deepest, darkest corners of the country. Over the years, it has reaped the rewards of making Coke available in more than 400,000 outlets across Indonesia's scattered islands.

But that kind of strategy, like the ability to buy mass television exposure, is simply not available to most companies. As a result, Indonesia has been one of the countries where marketers have been quick to latch on to the potential of Facebook. By 2015, there were already 70 million Indonesians using social media (a figure that's expected to rise to 98 million by 2018). But they weren't just being sociable. One study showed that half of all online purchases in Indonesia were made via Facebook.

In busy, compact, crowded, cosmopolitan Singapore, the challenges are different. But Zalora, a leading Singapore-based online fashion retailer, has made Facebook a central plank of its brand-building effort. From a standing start in 2012, the company reached a million orders in less than a year, and it went on to double the number of transactions and customers it handled by the end of 2014. It now serves Singapore, Malaysia, Indonesia, the Philippines, Thailand, Vietnam and Hong Kong, – and it's no coincidence that 30 per cent of its sales come from Malaysia, the country with the company's busiest and most popular Facebook page.

Zalora's brand-building philosophy is summed up by its managing director and co-founder, ex-Bain & Company consultant Tan Wee.

'There are a lot of online fashion retailers in Southeast Asia, but many people are still nervous about the business of buying online. We realised early on that we had to do something to differentiate ourselves and get over this lack of trust. Facebook gave us a platform to develop relationships with our customers. And as we all know, when you're in a relationship, you tend to trust people.

'Today, thanks to social media – and especially Twitter and Facebook – we can engage with those customers day and night. Using freely available tools, we can track our regular customers based on what they buy and how much they spend, how often they visit and what they like to wear.'

On a much more localised level, small businesses throughout Southeast Asia have found that Facebook enables them to build customer relationships like they never could before.

Geoff Siddle owns a chain of award-winning theme bars and restaurants that stretches right across Malaysia's affluent Klang Valley region. He uses Facebook to drive his marketing and retention strategies and to reach out to charities his customers like to get involved with.

'Historically, when customers were in my outlets my staff and I could build relationships with them and encourage them to come back,' he says.

'But as soon as they walked out of the door, all we could do was hope that they would come and see us again, preferably before too long. And hope, as New York's Mayor Rudy Giuliani said, is not a strategy. We did do some direct mail and advertising, but it was expensive and hard to measure.'

Facebook changed all that, and Geoff Siddle has found he can get a lot closer to his customers.

'The combination of low cost sales tools and a customer tracking system, plus the investment of a lot of our time to encourage people to interact with us on Facebook and share their experiences at our outlets, has helped us build a thriving community online,' he says.

'Most important of all, because we like and are friends with our customers on Facebook, we can find out where they are, what they are doing and what they are interested in. All we need to do is visit their Facebook pages. Used properly, but always confidentially, of course, we can time our messages to talk to them when they are online and to recognise their interests, their personal and professional milestones, their travel destinations and much, much more.

'This Facebook community means we can gain traction instantly when we want to generate interest in the many activities and events we organise, because every time someone likes, comments or shares one of our posts, their friends see it and share it some more.

'Nothing generates interest more than a picture of people

having fun – and we provide a place for people to have fun. With the help of Facebook, we can ensure the narrative continues to be developed.'

What's it about?

Here's the difficult bit. Using Facebook properly calls for imagination and ingenuity, and many firms can't quite get it right. Facebook is not about a single big idea. It's about a series of simple interactions that are often very small but very human. But all these tiny interactions add up to make your business part of the daily existence of people who have similar interests to the people who already spend money with you and interact with your business.

It's not just about personalised interactions with individuals, though. Facebook features powerful search tools that help consumers find personalised answers to a huge range of questions, giving businesses access to the kind of targeting they've always dreamed of.

For instance, if you key in 'nightclubs in Bangkok', you are presented with a list of nightclubs in Bangkok that have Facebook pages. Nothing groundbreaking there. You can get much the same list by putting the query into Google, Bing or other search engines. But Facebook's search takes this kind of enquiry to a new level. If you key in 'nightclubs in Bangkok that my friends have visited', you will see a personalised list of restaurants where your Facebook friends have eaten. And which is more likely to prompt you to go to a particular restaurant, an anonymous list or a list of restaurants people like you have chosen?

Another great Facebook search tool is 'Facebook Nearby'. This is a local search and discovery feature for Facebook Mobile apps that run on iPhones and Android smartphones.

'Facebook Nearby' allows users to search for specific places and businesses and see what's near them on a map, all assembled from friends' recommendations and check-ins.

With a bit of time and effort, these are the sort of tools that can build your business into a rock-solid company with a loyal and enthusiastic base of fans and customers.

Facebook is constantly innovating, with new products and services, some of which don't take off and some of which become hugely successful. To get the best out of it, you need to be sure that you and your community manager stay right on the ball and abreast of Facebook's new product offerings.

What's so good about it?

Imagine if a media owner came to you and said, 'I have a TV channel with 1.4 billion viewers – and I can tell you which of those 1.4 billion viewers match your specific target market. What's more, I can get you in front of them, not when they take a break but when they are engrossed in content that's related to what you are selling. Would you like to buy an ad?'

You'd bite that media owner's hand off, right?

But what if the media owner had even more to offer?

'It gets better. Not only can we do that, but we can match your budget, big or small. You tell us how much you want to spend and when you want to spend it and we'll work around that.'

You'd ask for that media owner's hand in marriage, right?

Well, that's what Facebook offers.

Facebook is a brilliant platform for engaging directly with your prospects, customers and other stakeholders. Used properly, it is a dynamic and inexpensive way to market, sell, build your narrative and stay close to your consumers.

It works for small, local businesses, but it can also be

exploited by much larger corporations, if they have the wit to behave in an informal, friendly, non-corporate way. Red Bull is an enormous worldwide company, a US$7 billion giant with 10,000 employees, but it spends very little on traditional advertising. Instead, it has invested a lot of effort in its social media initiatives and it now has 44 million likes on Facebook – more than Britney Spears and almost as many as David Beckham. Its Facebook page is packed with photos, games, apps, events and chat about anything and everything related to the brand. In a market where it's very easy to slap together a generic energy drink containing caffeine, taurine and sugar and sell it at half the price of the market leader, Red Bull has built a brand that inspires huge loyalty and guarantees its ability to sell profitably in 166 different countries. And right there, at the heart of its brand strategy, is Facebook.

What's not so good about it?

Maintaining a Facebook page for your business isn't a one-off tactical initiative. You need to keep content on Facebook current, interesting, dynamic, accurate and truthful, contributing to relevant discussions and engaging other brands and consumers. While advertising often allows businesses to get away with being economical with the truth, Facebook is so transparent that if you lie you'll get found out and shown up very quickly indeed.

One of the most popular metrics that's used to assess the success of a Facebook page is the number of likes it has. Unfortunately, as is so often the case when something is successful, there is an almost irresistible temptation to game the system. You can buy Facebook likes, generated artificially by automated bots, for about US$18 per thousand. And it is not only fly-by-night companies that have cheated like this, in their attempts to look popular and on the ball. One major Southeast Asian airline was widely mocked online when it appeared to attract a phenomenal one million likes in a suspiciously short time. Anyone who is interested in finding out how real an apparently popular company's Facebook likes are has only to use one of the online forensic tools like Yelp or Status Counter to check their authenticity.

This is an important consideration for younger businesses that are looking to grow fast and then go public, and that might be tempted to cut corners. Institutions that were vastly impressed by social media stats just a year or two ago will now make a point of rigorously evaluating both the numbers and the quality of a firm's social media network during their due diligence efforts.

Facebook, of course, is well aware of the danger of faked likes undermining the value of real ones. It now has an ingenious automatic monitoring system that analyses the levels of engagement with your page to decide how exciting your content really is and how many fans should see it. If you have tens of thousands of inactive users, that will actually reduce the amount of exposure Facebook gives your content.

Who should use Facebook?

Facebook is not an optional extra. You can't afford not to be on it. But you do need to use it properly. For businesses of all sizes, creating and maintaining a Facebook page is an excellent, cost-effective way to provide current, relevant information to your customers and humanise the brand. It gives people a chance to get to know you and to build a relationship with your brand, become a part of it and encourage their friends to get involved as well. In the old days, this was called word-of-mouth recommendation, and it was accepted as the best of all possible forms of marketing.

By establishing a transparent narrative on Facebook, you are giving your customers the opportunity to interact and engage with your brand and personally recommend it to others. Ultimately, if the content you post is interesting or odd enough, there is just a chance that it may go viral, as friends pass it on to friends and they relay it to their friends and so on around the world.

You can't bank on that, because it's way beyond anyone's control. But you can certainly maximise your chances of winning likes and shares, followers and friends on Facebook. And that will boost your sales. The trick is to be accessible, creative and cheerful, use humour and lateral thinking and generally make sure your content reflects your company's human personality, rather than a dull, grey corporate monotone.

Who shouldn't use Facebook?

No-one really. Every kind of business can find a way to make use of the opportunities it has created. Even the world's abattoirs, whaling fleets and fracking companies can use Facebook to tell their side of the story, engage consumers and shed light on what, I'm sure, are terribly misunderstood industries.

All right, how do I get started?

Facebook offers an impressive amount of detailed help and advice for businesses on its website. So the first thing you and your community manager need to do is go to the Facebook for Business section of the site, where there's an easy-to-follow five-step process for setting up your Facebook page.

You will need a Facebook Business page, because there are strict limits on what can and can't be done with a personal page on Facebook. You can't advertise it, for example. And there's a limit on the number of friends you can have on a non-business page, which rather defeats the purpose.

Once your Facebook Business page is set up, you'll need to get down to work and start building your audience. Start by emailing customers, partners, suppliers and others and inviting them to visit the page. Link your Facebook Business page to your company website, your blog and any other social profiles you may have. Don't forget to become a fan of your own Facebook page and suggest your friends visit it and like it. You should also put a link to it in all your email signatures and add it to business cards. Facebook is constantly changing and adding new features, month by month, so the best approach is to visit the Facebook for Business first steps pages and see what is most relevant to your needs.

If you are also building a presence on Twitter – and you definitely should – use the Twitter account to announce your new business page, but don't keep on tweeting about it. Instead, create compelling content to share across Twitter that links back to your Facebook page. And don't forget to thank those who share your tweets.

If you have an e-newsletter, use the content you create for Facebook in the e-newsletter as well. Remember, too, to post links from your e-newsletter back to content on the Facebook business page.

When you comment on a third-party post or an industry-related forum or blog, link back to your Facebook Business page. Also share, write about and post comments on business developments in your industry, case studies or white papers you have produced and relevant books or ebooks you have come across.

When you put up new content or comment on other

people's content, you start a dialogue. Hopefully, other people will comment on what you've posted. This is your opportunity. Get involved in the conversation. Develop it, pick up on the points other people are making and take them further. This interaction, this involvement in the developing conversation, is the whole point of doing what you are doing. You can't just go through the motions, pumping out a crude selling message like you would in an advert. You have to get stuck in, respond to other people's views and gradually, organically, build an online personality for your brand. It's not about *doing* social; it's about *being* social.

Facebook has given you access to these amazing virtual rooms with well over a billion people in them. You are right there with them and the crowd of people you are engaging with is growing and you are slowly creating a community of people interested in what you do.

If you are genuine, human, interesting and transparent, this network will grow and grow, as long as you make the effort to feed it. The days of spending colossal amounts of money on mass advertising are over. Facebook has a massive database of current and relevant information about users. And it's yours for free. It's time to take advantage of it.

'People who find your Pinterest boards stay engaged with your brand for longer.

The average visitor spends roughly a quarter of an hour on the site, far more than the time spent on Facebook and Twitter combined'

CHAPTER 19

Can You Get the World Pinterested?

So far, I've mainly been talking about Facebook, Twitter, YouTube and LinkedIn, the big beasts in the social media jungle. But they are not the only platforms that are worth exploring. Instagram, for example, is growing quite quickly in SE Asia, certainly for sharing personal content. But it is Pinterest that offers one of the better options for businesses, especially since the introduction of its Buyable Pins button, launched in late 2015.

What is it?

Pinterest is a straightforward and intuitive photo sharing website, based on visual bookmarks known as 'pins'. When you come across an image you like, you can 'pin' it in seconds, effectively sticking it up on a virtual pinboard where others can share your discovery. Pinterest gives people and businesses – or businesses and people – the opportunity to connect up via their shared interests, tastes and passions. It's a highly visual tool that focuses on discovering, storing and sharing other people's images, rather your own. That makes it particularly important for companies with a visual product to sell.

Who uses it?

The user numbers are big. Pinterest has 100 million users and counting, 85 per cent of them female – though it reported 120 per cent growth in the number of male users in 2015. On the consumer side, that predominantly female appeal means it is ideal for anyone offering a visually compelling product to women. Pew Research reports that nearly 68 per cent of users have an income of over US$75,000, which makes it an unusually responsive medium for those in the travel, holiday and luxury goods sectors, car manufacturers and property developers. The figures compare well with Instagram, which has more, but poorer, users. Only half of all Instagram users have an income of over US$50,000.

Edison Foo, founder of Singapore investment property broker Newlaunch101.com, began using Pinterest in early 2013. Foo hasn't got the budget to match his competitors, the big international real estate firms. But he has made a splash out of all proportion to his resources, thanks to an energetic social media strategy that integrates many different platforms to create maximum exposure for the properties on his books.

Nadiah Kimie, COO of start-up online fashion retailer FiftySeven, based in Kuala Lumpur, has spent a long time tracking down the data and working out how to make Pinterest a main plank of the new company's marketing. She knows the visual appeal of her products will echo the visual appeal of Pinterest's pinboards. But she's also made a note of the cold, hard facts.

'Average order value for products on Pinterest is higher than Google, Yahoo, Bing, Facebook, Twitter and even Amazon,' she says.

'According to our research, the average order value generated by Pinterest is US$169, compared with US$95 for Facebook and US$71 for Twitter. I've seen figures from

Shopify that say that 93% of Pinterest users are looking for something to buy, so you can take it from me that Pinterest will be playing a major role in how we market the products on our site.'

What's it about?

Pinterest consists of virtual pinboards where you can collect images from the web, organise them and add comments specifically related to your requirements, explaining why the image is important and what you want to do with it or how it inspires you.

The most successful boards tend to be very focused and specific. They include boards dedicated to graphic design and brand identities, home office designs, sugar-free desserts, unique birthday gifts for kids, biker jackets, 'Books I Want to Read', favourite places and architecture, new homes and lots of recipes, from vegan desserts and cajun favourites to secrets of a better mojito.

What's so good about it?

Because of its visual nature and the fact that visitors tend to be interested in what you are offering (otherwise, why would they be there?), people who find your Pinterest boards stay engaged with your brand for longer. In fact, the average visitor spends roughly a quarter of an hour on the site, far more than the time spent on Facebook and Twitter combined.

Pinterest is the source of 5.5 per cent of all referral traffic to business sites of any sort. That is hugely more than the combined total for YouTube, Google+ and LinkedIn and is only bettered by Facebook. More significantly still,

Pinterest claims a staggering 23% share of all direct referrals to e-commerce sites. In other words, nearly one in four of all referrals from social media for online shopping comes from Pinterest.

It's a clean, uncluttered, simple-looking site, with a powerful search engine, and people don't need to put in a lot of effort to find their way around. Images are the main attraction, and the quality tends to be very high. Comments are minimal and any 'Action' buttons are hidden so they only appear when you scroll over them.

It's easy to use and if you load the 'Pin It' browser plug-in, you can post new content on Pinterest even when you aren't on the site.

What's not so good about it?

At the moment, Pinterest is very US-centred, with nearly half of all users in North America. But that's changing, as its worldwide growth continues (global traffic up 125 per cent in 2013, though it levelled out somewhat in 2014), opening up plenty of early adopter opportunities in Asian markets. In Southeast Asia, it's most popular in the Philippines and Malaysia, but much less well-known in Vietnam and Singapore.

Pinterest has a few clones in Asia, particularly in Vietnam, but none of them has achieved high levels of penetration, apart from Mogujie and Meilishuo, which seem to have cornered the market in China.

Who should use Pinterest?

Pinterest will work well for architects, property developers, real estate agents, interior decorators, graphic designers (and just about any other designer), hotels, food and beverage outlets (nice ones, anyway), fashion and clothing firms, luxury goods companies, freelance models, musicians, inventors, educators – anyone whose products or services have a strong visual element or where being able to present an attractive and human face is going to encourage contact and enquiries.

Who shouldn't use Pinterest?

There are some organisations that should definitely steer clear of Pinterest. 'Bad news' businesses and those that generate disturbing imagery have to handle all their social media activity with great care and tact, but need to be especially careful with the most visual media. That means all those abattoirs, pharmaceutical research companies, surgeons, oil and gas companies (especially those involved in fracking and shale gas) and Japanese whaling firms should probably try a different, less visually-oriented approach. They'll be better off sticking to Facebook.

All right, how do I get started?

The great thing with all the top social media sites, including Pinterest, is that they tend to have excellent online tutorials. So even if you don't yet employ a community manager, it shouldn't take you long to learn how you can put it to work. Start off by doing a bit of research. Spend some time looking around and watch out for your competitors and brands with similar offerings. Work out what catches your eye and why it makes you want to engage with the image. And once you've got a feel for that, don't be afraid to mimic what works. See what is being repinned and make sure your images are up to the same high standard. That moody, grainy lowlight pic you took on your smartphone might be good enough for Facebook (though that's debatable). It certainly won't cut it on Pinterest.

See if your customers are using Pinterest. How are they using it? What seems to work, and what doesn't? If you're lucky enough to have a highly visual product or service, like interior design, make sure you add a 'Pin It' button to your website to make it easy for customers to pin items there that catch their fancy.

And when you upload an image, don't forget to edit the pin to add a link. Pinterest doesn't automatically add a link to the image, and you don't want to miss out on what could be a great marketing opportunity.

Be imaginative. If you are a retailer, don't create boards that are just about your store. Instead, create boards related to the value you can give to specific customer segments.

A retailer like Isetan, the Japanese department store with branches across the capital cities of Asia, might decide to create boards such as 'Summer Weddings at Isetan'. Kare, the German furniture company, sells its products around the world, from Munich to Moscow, from Athens to Accra. But customers in Southeast Asia need very different furniture from those in chilly Northern Europe, so it would make sense for Kare to create a board that showed a range of ideas for hot climates. Setting up a board called 'The Perfect Tropical Living Room' could be done in a few hours and would certainly generate pins and boost sales, at virtually no cost.

Create lots of boards and make sure they are all 'key word ready'. Think in terms of locations, events, themes and lifestyles – and then come up with relevant and specific key words that will help interested people find your boards easily. A board called 'My Favourite Cities', for instance, will not be half as effective as 'Bangkok River Markets'.

Although Pinterest is very visual, you can also post news,

ideas, tips – anything that might be useful or interesting to the kind of people you want to be talking to. You might even decide you wanted to include good products from companies with a similar offering (although you might also want to make sure these companies are from the other side of the world!). Stay within the conventions of Pinterest and keep text captions short to avoid annoying users.

Finally, remember that Pinterest is not a soapbox that's been put there so that you can shout your wares and thump your branding chest. It is a social media platform, and social media conversations are built on two-way traffic. Make sure you play your part and contribute regularly to the community and the conversation by commenting on, liking, sharing and re-pinning other people's images.

SECTION 4

What Will a Brand Consultant Do for You?

'A rigorous, disciplined, warts-and-all brand healthcheck is the one sure way of knowing what's right about what you're doing, what's wrong and what can be improved.

Once you know these things in detail, you can take action that's prioritised, purposeful and cost-effective'

CHAPTER 20

What Is Your Brand Really Saying?

Overall, business in Southeast Asia has had it pretty good for the last couple of decades. Countries like Malaysia have seen plenty of years of strong growth, with only the occasional temporary blip. Surging demand has provided opportunities for local companies to expand and build market share in a business environment that was often so benign they could even get away with making mistakes now and again.

But that is all changing now. As SE Asian countries become wealthier and the middle classes grow, our markets are becoming more and more attractive to the big global brands. Overseas companies that either ignored SE Asia altogether or made half-hearted attempts to move in on our regional markets are getting their act together and coming back to do it properly. The various ASEAN Economic Community proposals and global trade pacts are not going to change the world overnight, but their long-term effects will certainly include promoting fiercer competition. Times are going to get tougher. The competition is getting smarter. And local companies are going to have to become smarter and more professional about building their brands, selling their products and looking after their customers.

That's the bad news.

The good news is that changing technologies, and particularly the internet and social media, are giving them new and affordable ways to fight back against the apparently limitless spending power and advertising budgets of their international competitors. Trying to slug it out toe to toe, matching a big global brand dollar for dollar, campaign for campaign, is not going to work. There can only be one winner in this kind of duel – and it won't be the company that's based in KL or Singapore or Jakarta.

Just ask Creative Technologies, of Singapore, whose highly-rated Nomad digital audio players were often considered better than the iPod. Despite winning a lawsuit against Apple and deploying a US$100m advertising budget, the regional high-tech heroes never stood a chance against the American behemoth.

The advice embodied in the title of this book, to stop advertising and start branding, is the key to getting it right and ensuring success over the next five to ten years.

Marketing strategies based on massive advertising firepower and repeated mass media ad campaigns are the equivalent of mounting a head-on assault with a conventional army, using tanks and artillery and vast infantry battalions. SE Asian businesses need to find other ways to fight – and the tactics that will work for them are going to be much more like those of guerrilla warfare.

It all starts with knowing the territory, knowing the people and knowing the technology – and how to use it to help build relationships and win hearts and minds. In the business context, engaging with your customers, listening to them and addressing their concerns, responding to their needs and winning their long-term loyalty will be the key factors.

But how do you start to do this effectively, if you don't have a clear and objective view of your brand's reason for being, its position in the market and your own strengths and weaknesses? Few companies anywhere have this kind of clarity, and SE Asian companies, often family-owned or dominated by a single dynamic and sometimes autocratic leader, are particularly bad at achieving objectivity. And that is one very good reason why commissioning a rigorous and professional brand audit is such an important step in preparing your business for the tough times ahead.

Brand audit projects aren't glamorous. Ad agencies that will pull out all the stops just to get the chance to pitch for a big account tend to go very quiet if you try to talk to them about the hard, down-to-earth work of auditing exactly where your brand stands and how well it is delivering on its promises to customers. They're probably right to be bashful, too. They aren't really equipped to do this kind of work. They'd much rather spend their time dreaming up dazzling new commercials or witty slogans and persuading their clients to pour more and more money into multimedia campaigns. Brand audits take time, skill and effort, and you have to know exactly what you're looking for.

But they are probably the single most valuable tool there is when it comes to helping a company decide what it needs to do, where it should be investing and how it should be focusing its efforts. They have become a key part of my business at Fusionbrand, simply because they provide so much valuable information and so many clear hints as to how to build and sustain a brand without spending a fortune to do it.

Welcome to the brand healthcheck

The problem is, of course, that the phrase 'brand audit' is about as exciting as a wet weekend in Medan.

No-one's going to get worked up about the need for a process that sounds so dull and uninspiring and that gives no real clue as to what is involved and what the benefits might be. So I've taken to calling this auditing process a 'brand healthcheck' – which at least gives some clearer idea of what we will be doing and why it might be important.

In fact, when it comes to it, this comprehensive look at every aspect of the brand's status and performance is anything but a dreary accounting process. What we're doing is taking the temperature of the brand and assessing its fitness for the commercial battles ahead.

It's something every business should do, and it's certainly not an academic exercise. The people we work with almost always find that it throws up a string of practical ideas for cutting costs, understanding and serving customers better and making the business more efficient.

One recent client summed it up neatly.

'The dozens of recommendations that emerged from the brand healthcheck you did for us have helped us improve our communications, our present performance and our future planning,' he wrote enthusiastically.

'You've saved us money straight away by highlighting activities that were ineffective and needed to be scrapped. Even on that level, the brand healthcheck has probably paid for itself three times over.

'More to the point, though, the recommendations have shown us how we can save perhaps half of our advertising budget in the next year or two – and put some of that money to work on activities that really will delight our existing customers, generate highly-qualified leads and give our brand strength in depth.'

We have seen this kind of reaction time and time again. Organisations almost always benefit from an instant payback on their investment in a brand healthcheck, simply because the detailed, forensic investigation into what is really going on strips away opinions and assumptions and pinpoints opportunities for immediate improvements and savings.

The longer-term benefits, which can sometimes be as

radical as a new approach to an organisation's entire business model or a wholesale shift in the way marketing budgets are used, effectively come free. That makes a brand healthcheck just about the best investment any company or public sector organisation can undertake. Alongside our commercial clients, we have done a lot of great work with government departments and agencies that need to engage with their citizens, helping them understand people's perceptions of them, assess their ability to deliver value and improve their reputations.

But what does a brand healthcheck actually involve? What are the objectives? And how does it go about achieving them?

The basic aim is to take stock of your brand's current situation and set a benchmark against which future progress can be measured. This means taking an unflinching look at where the brand is, what stakeholders inside and outside the organisation really think of it and want from it, what you are doing right (and wrong) at each brand touchpoint, who influences your customers and what channels are most likely to reach and engage them.

Brand healthcheck reports can be uncomfortable reading. They can even deliver shocks, as they can often uncover major disconnects between what a company believes its brand to be and what the customers think about it. As I have said so many times before, we live in a world, now, where it's the customer, not the 'brand owner', who determines the success of the brand.

I remember the advertising campaign, a while ago, for Proton's new MPV, the Exora, which the Malaysian carmaker desperately tried to convince us was 'amazing'. That was dumb marketing in itself, as it gave an immediate hostage to fortune. Even if the new Proton model was, by any standards, a bit amazing, what did that make other cars on the road – the BMWs and Audis, the Ferraris and Lamborghinis, the top-of-the-range S-class Mercedes or the mighty Rolls-Royce?

The consumer reaction was understandably sceptical. Did consumers believe for one minute that the new Proton would be, in any sense, amazing? No. Did they fail to notice that the company was going way over the top in its efforts to hype up a bit of frothy excitement about its rather ordinary new MPV? No. They noticed. Were they impressed? No.

Did the campaign manage to erase their long-term memories of being stuck behind Proton taxis at toll booths, year after year, while the drivers opened the doors to pass the money out, because Proton's electric windows always seemed to have broken down? Nope. It's probably 15 years or more since Proton managed to fix the window motor problem, but the number of cars with permanently stuck windows only seems to taper down gradually, and the stigma is still there. That's actually something of a backhanded tribute to the longevity of some of the older Protons, something a shrewd marketer might have found a way to pick up on. But, of course, no-one did. After all, no ad agency is going to win those coveted awards for copy about fixing an awkward legacy issue like that.

Any serious attempt at a brand healthcheck – and companies will sometimes try to launch these exercises using internal staff, though I would strongly recommend them to think twice before setting up a team that will inevitably lack the objective outsider's impartial eye – would quickly have warned Proton's senior management of the derision that would inevitably follow the launch of the 'amazing' Exora. Whatever people working for Proton thought their brand represented, it was the voice of the public that was chuckling over the hype about the underwhelming newcomer.

Ignorance can be fatal. An organisation that insults the intelligence of consumers and doesn't understand the realities of its situation stands no chance of taking control of its destiny. A rigorous, disciplined, warts-and-all brand healthcheck is the one sure way of knowing what's right about where you are, what you're doing, what's wrong and what can be improved. Once you know these things in detail, you can take action that's prioritised, purposeful and cost-effective.

The brand healthcheck – three key elements

In practice, a brand healthcheck consists of three essential elements, each of which throws light on a particular aspect of the brand's strengths and weaknesses:

1. An **internal brand audit**, based on a combination of one-to-one interviews and surveys with executives, managers and front-line staff, uncovers knowledge gaps related to the brand and reveals attitudes to customers and other stakeholders. It looks at the brand's values, vision and mission and assesses whether they resonate with the environment the organisation operates in. It explores whether staff members understand them and how their actions impact those brand values and it examines the way the company's people and processes relate to and interact with the outside world.

2. A **communications audit** covers the brand identity, how data is collected and used, internal communications, advertising and PR, websites, logos, brochures and the brand's social media presence. It analyses the relevance and effectiveness of all the ways the company uses to promote itself and its messages and engage with consumers and customers.

3. An **external brand audit** assesses the company and the brand from the point of view of all the important external stakeholders – customers (including lost customers), prospects, distributors and retailers, suppliers, media and

regulators. It looks at the interactions and experiences these stakeholders have with the brand and feeds back a wealth of information about their real perceptions of it and what can be done to improve these perceptions.

When these three elements are set side by side, they often expose dangerous discrepancies between the CEO's view of the situation and the reality that exists on the ground. These discrepancies may have arisen because of unrealistic assumptions, incompetence, lack of oversight, faulty data and systems or even sheer bad luck. But they may also be the result of individuals turning a blind eye to problems they should be tackling head on, or even of people deliberately misleading their superiors and painting a falsely rosy picture of the brand's position in the market.

All too often, our brand audit teams find that the generally positive views they hear from people inside the company bear no relation to the views they collect from the external stakeholders.

We've seen this happen so frequently that it no longer surprises us. Yet many companies (and agencies, too) still fail to recognise the vital importance of the internal work that forms part of a comprehensive brand healthcheck. I've seen so-called brand audits that neglect this inexpensive but essential ground work and focus entirely on a company's marketing campaigns, leaving it vulnerable to all kinds of delusions and misunderstandings about the realities of its situation.

The first stage, the internal brand audit, is the starting place for everything that follows. It begins with confidential interviews with directors, managers and staff, across different departments, asking them about their perceptions of the brand, the branding goals behind it, corporate and brand messages, and the company's past branding activities. It looks at customer processes, sales and service performance, and the ways customer data is collected, analysed, shared and used.

The brief survey questionnaires generally take around ten minutes to complete and focus on perceptions, value and understanding of the brand. The face-to-face interviews each take up to 45 minutes, starting off with a list of prepared topics and guidelines but developing into the kind of free-ranging discussion that can often deliver the most important insights of all. Their success is crucially dependent on the skill and ingenuity of the interviewer, who will use a number of different techniques to elicit the subtler, more nuanced views and ideas of each interviewee. For example, there are certain provocative questions we ask in order to trigger more imaginative responses than people are used to providing. For example:

'Imagine it is five years from now and you and the company are celebrating historic levels of financial and market success.

'How did the organisation get to this high point? When you look back on the previous years, what are the activities that have underpinned these triumphs? What have you done, and not done, to make the brand loved by your customers and profitable for you?'

The experienced interviewer's broad toolkit of questions and techniques virtually guarantees that unexpected views and insights will emerge. The more people are interviewed – from the CEO and the financial director to the receptionist in the office and the helpline worker, the bookkeeper, the maintenance man and the delivery driver – the more detail will be captured about how the company really thinks and works. Even if time, cost and other constraints make it impossible to talk to as many people as you ideally would, the internal brand audit is still vitally important. A well planned survey questionnaire, backed up by just ten, or even half a dozen, interviews, spread across the different functions and levels within the company, will often produce startling insights that can form the basis for action.

Why would you want to talk to the maintenance man or the bookkeeper responsible for accounts payable? They are not usually seen as part of the branding process. But the fact is that even the maintenance man will occasionally be in direct contact with customers or suppliers. He will be the person closing the exhibition hall at the end of the day. It will be his reaction, when people say 'Oh, please, can you give us just five more minutes?', that determines whether they go away thinking the company is helpful and flexible or staffed by grumpy, time-serving people who put their own interests first. The accounts payable clerk can help keep suppliers happy by paying bills on time or drive them round the bend by stalling and holding payments back.

Companies that are slow to pay their bills – whether because of slackness, accounting problems or cashflow difficulties – don't inspire confidence. They may even find it harder to get credit from suppliers. Rumours can start all too easily. A CEO who is struggling to make sure everyone in every part of the organisation is on brand and projecting the same values is not going to welcome calls from important suppliers about unpaid bills. It is a key part of the value of the brand healthcheck that it can uncover the answers to so many of these questions that are never normally asked.

The truth is this: your brand's reputation is in the hands of your people – all of them, all the time.

People need to know what they have to do. But they need to combine this with an understanding of how and why they are doing it a particular way and how that relates to the overall values and identity of the brand.

To put it another way, a brand – any brand – is built from the inside out.

That's why sheer weight of advertising and creative ingenuity, the traditional tools of the big marketers, are not the answer. They may produce a spike in sales when spending is at its peak, but they are not enough to breathe life into a brand and give it sustainable momentum.

The next stage, the communications audit, is especially important for larger firms, where there may be several divisions or departments involved in branding activities and mixed messages are often an obvious problem.

If the people in charge of the company's communications don't know, with absolute clarity, exactly what the brand values and messages are, they will not be singing from the same hymn sheet. It's not surprising customers and consumers get confused, if an airline, for example, tries to be all things to all men and ends up positioning itself as a luxury dream carrier one day and a cheap-as-chips no-frills budget brand the next.

For all those who believe I'm in the habit of picking on Malaysia Airlines for its abysmal marketing and communication performance over the past few years, I would like to point out that I am naming no names here. We could be talking about any badly-run airline that showed a consistent inability to choose a clear, credible strategy and stick to it. Any airline at all. Like Malaysia Airlines, for example. (Incidentally, I am not dishonouring the dead, or belittling the dreadful tragedy of the two MAS disasters in 2014 in any way when I point out the inept handling of the airline's business. I have been flying with MAS for decades, and I don't intend to stop now. But there is no reason at all why poor management, a culture of mediocrity and unprofessional marketing over many years should be entitled to a free pass and exemption from all critical comment because of these unrelated horrors.)

Your communications audit must be honest and comprehensive. It needs to examine all the visual material and messaging that represents your brand, including the brand identity, ad campaigns, press releases, brochures, websites and other online activities. It should be covering everything from 40-foot billboards to email signatures and everything in between. It needs to take a critical look at all these elements, in isolation, and at the level of consistency and integration between them.

Do they present a single, coherent picture? Do they say the same things? Are your messages relevant to the target audiences and geographical markets they are aimed at? Do they communicate a genuine and believable set of corporate values and standards? Does the content you generate do what it's supposed to do? Is it shared effectively, using the right channels? Have you recruited influencers who can help you spread the word?

Most companies have a brand manual that is aimed at setting communication benchmarks and enforcing consistency. Does this provide the guidance needed to ensure that people in different departments and roles speak with one voice? And how effectively is the company tapping into the potential of social media, currently the most powerful and cost-effective way for SE Asian businesses to establish and grow their brands?

Building a social media presence that will build the brand organically and foster wider, deeper two-way relationships with potential and existing customers calls for specialised skills that are quite different from those in the traditional marketing communications armoury. These skills are in short supply in SE Asia, but this is not an issue any ambitious company can ignore. The challenges have to be addressed, understood and eventually seen as the opportunities they really are.

The most powerful elements in the social media armoury – Facebook, Twitter, LinkedIn, Instagram, Pinterest and TripAdvisor and the multitude of other review and comparison sites – must all be considered. Does the brand have a presence in these key places? Which platforms are relevant to your industry and your brand? There is no rule that says a company should be equally active in all the different social media contexts, but it should have a strategy that includes using the right social media vehicles for particular functions, such as customer service responses, communicating with frequent flyers and taking the sting out of unfounded rumours or unfair criticisms. The communications audit will analyse both policy and practice in this area, and invariably generates specific recommendations about how to build better online relationships with customers and strengthen the brand.

The third and last element, the external brand audit, is usually the most expensive and time-consuming part of the brand healthcheck exercise. It can also be the most rewarding. It involves finding and talking to customers, lost customers and potential buyers, suppliers, and distributors and retailers. It should also include conversations with early adopters, journalists and bloggers whose writings influence public opinion, and, where applicable, with governments and regulatory authorities. These are the people whose opinions the company needs to know and understand, because, between them, they define what the brand really means in the world, rather than what it claims or hopes to signify.

All these external stakeholder groups have a part to play in deciding the brand's destiny and – importantly – none of them is under the company's direct control. If the researchers can find the right people and persuade them to give the exercise their time and attention, these should be the most revealing interviews of all. We will always make sure we talk to several groups of customers – actual, potential and lost ('When and why did you move away and what would it take to win you back?'). If possible, we will also conduct interviews with a sample of competitors' customers. Though these conversations are sometimes hard to set up, they can provide uniquely relevant insights into our client's brand and its strengths and weaknesses.

Again, each face-to-face conversation will begin with

a sequence of fairly standard questions, developing and branching out as it goes on.

Typical questions for customers include 'Why did you buy from us the first time?', 'Why did you choose us over a competitor?', 'What can we do to improve our customer support?' and 'How can we improve our company's relationship with you?'

Suppliers will be asked about the company's responsiveness, its characteristics as a trading partner and even how readily and promptly it pays its bills. Occasionally, though, the interviewer will throw in a rather less conventional question, in the hope of gaining some new perspectives on the situation. We will sometimes even invite interviewees to imagine they were in our clients' shoes.

'If you were running the company, what one thing would you change so that it would be better at meeting your requirements?' we ask.

The answers, spontaneous, often slightly surprising, sometimes completely unexpected, can spark whole new ideas for future products, services and content – or even suggest better, occasionally cheaper, ways of doing the things the company already does.

Meeting these external stakeholders face to face is always the best way to dig around and explore the nuances of their opinions. But the costs involved necessarily mean that this in-depth qualitative research will be limited by the budget that is available. The traditional survey technique of intercepts – short interviews with people stopped in the street – also has its part to play. But it is now possible to get the views of much larger samples, quickly and cheaply, through internet research tools. Using tools like Survey Monkey, Fusionbrand can now carry out a 500-respondent survey in less than two weeks, rather than three months, at a price any organisation can afford. It takes some expertise to get the questions just right, but our online surveys are regularly producing useful and informative comments – and above-average response rates of 8 per cent or so, which don't happen unless you've succeeded in engaging people.

Apart from collecting the opinions of all the external stakeholders, it is important to carry out some objective testing to examine the interactions that are creating their good or bad perceptions of your brand. The external brand audit will usually include experiential research in which audit team members pose as prospects or customers and record their impressions of the service and follow-up they receive from sales, marketing and customer support staff, in retail outlets or at trade shows, on the telephone and in response to email requests for information. To put this into context, the researchers will also approach competing brands with similar queries or requests and compare the quality of service your competitors provide.

In practice, this can yield vast amounts of valuable detail. But, again, the researcher needs a sophisticated understanding of what he is looking for. It takes a lot of experience to know who to approach and what questions to ask and to assess the responses.

When working with an investment and development authority in SE Asia, for example, we posed as representatives of an international site selection firm gathering data about investment locations in the region. We judged the quality of each interaction in terms of responsiveness, empathy and ability to provide the information we asked for, examined the speed, relevance and tone of any correspondence that ensued and tracked any follow-up activity our calls had generated. For comparison purposes, we also collected similar information from five other economic development zones, including direct competitors such as Iskandar Malaysia and the Sharjah Investment and Development Authority (Shurooq).

The results of this fieldwork showed, as usually happens, that there was plenty of scope for improvement, including many minor changes that could be made quickly and at little or no cost.

Detailed investigations like this help to pinpoint the differences between what people say – or even genuinely think – they do and what actually happens in the heat of the moment.

This kind of perception gap can only be addressed through improving operational excellence. Advertising won't do it. Indeed, if your advertising promises something and the customer experience delivers something far worse, your brand's reputation can be shattered.

I've already mentioned the famous Bain & Co study that revealed 80 per cent of companies believed they delivered superior customer service – and the gaping chasm between this 80 per cent figure and the 8 per cent of companies that the customers themselves felt delivered exceptional service.

That delivery gap is a good example of the kind of painful delusion the comprehensive brand healthcheck process is designed to drag out into the spotlight. You could see the whole brand healthcheck, in academic terms, as a perception gap study. But this is not an academic exercise. It's a practical, down-to-earth way of focusing a company's efforts on what it needs to do to survive and thrive.

The experience is everything

Once the results of the three audit elements – internal, communications and external – have been analysed and compared with each other, it is almost always possible to identify a range of short- and long-term improvements the company could make, often at no additional cost. Many of the most significant changes, in terms of improving customer perceptions and staff attitudes and performance, are likely to be the kind of detailed adjustments that appear unspectacular in themselves but build up to create a powerful and positive cumulative impact on your brand.

For example, service and support staff may have been convinced they were already doing a good job. They were in the right place at the right time. They answered customer queries and carried out whatever tasks their managers had told them to.

But if the external brand audit interviews reveal that real customers found their manner rude or unhelpful and their product knowledge gappy, this is information that managers need to take on board and act on.

Blindness to the outsider's view of the brand and the company is a perennial weakness in organisations of all sizes. The brand healthcheck's ability to present the internal view and the external stakeholders' perspectives side by side – and to compare and contrast them to identify what needs to be improved – provides a unique opportunity. The customer may not even be right in every case, but that's not the point.

The experience really is everything. Nothing is more important in business today than the task of getting the organisation ready to deliver an outstanding experience for consumers, so that they will come back time and time again.

This is not easy. Experiences related to the brand must be consistent and they must resonate with consumers and customers on many different levels, including intangible factors such as the 'new car smell'. Apple, for example, has identified the moment of opening its product packaging as a key point in the buyer's experience of the brand. The sale has already been made, of course, but Apple is already looking forward to the next sale in a couple of years' time. It has spent millions on optimising the look, and even the feel, of its packaging to heighten the pleasure of that first meeting with your new Mac or iPhone.

If visitors to your company's showrooms or offices feel the staff there are offhand, that will have a negative effect on the brand, whether or not it's true. But there are plenty of minor low-cost initiatives managers can take that will start to change that customer perception. Introducing or updating uniforms may be appropriate in some contexts. Reorganising shopfloor and point of sale processes so that people look busier and more purposeful could have a disproportionate impact. Even half an hour's training every now and then to get front-line staff into the habit of making eye contact and listening patiently to customers' questions and grumbles before trying to come up with answers can make a difference.

Among all the other benefits that flow from investing in a rigorous, professional brand healthcheck, the biggest single payoff is usually the knowledge that you are making your plans from a position of strength, knowing the truth about your brand and the world it operates in. Good information and shrewd recommendations will help you play to your strengths and rectify your weaknesses, so that the money you spend can generate the greatest possible impact.

In the end, most of what we're suggesting is about getting back to basics, doing the things businesses have always had to do, but taking advantage of the newest tools and technologies to do them better – and often more cheaply.

'Knowledge itself is power,' said Francis Bacon, back in 1597. He was right then, and he's even righter today. Two thousand years earlier, an inscription in the Temple of Apollo at Delphi told the Ancient Greeks the key to success was to 'Know thyself'.

That's what a brand healthcheck can give you. And if you want my two-penn'orth, I'll just quote you the old American Express slogan. Don't leave home without it.

'The brand blueprint can help the CEO step back and relinquish many of the more detailed tasks of day-to-day management, while still retaining control'

CHAPTER 21

Creating the Blueprint for Success

If the brand healthcheck is the key to knowing the truth about your brand today, the brand blueprint is the roadmap that charts the way forward.

But a brand blueprint is not like any traditional business plan. Instead of being the usual mass of guesses and spreadsheet projections, leading to increasingly fanciful predictions about the financial results the organisation may or may not achieve two, three or five years out, the brand blueprint focuses on one key fact that will not be affected by market fluctuations, new competition, exchange rates or changing technologies.

The brand blueprint doesn't give you hopeful forecasts of sales or profit figures for the years to come. What it does give you is a guarantee that if you put it into practice and successfully build and nurture your brand, you will be firmly on the right road and able to cope with any shocks and surprises that come your way.

A conventional business plan is always, inevitably, based on the assumption that the company dictates the brand and that things will proceed much as they are today – plus or minus the odd market trend here or the odd economic downturn there. It can't foresee what is to come, or prepare you for unexpected and disruptive change.

But a good brand blueprint will map out where the brand

needs to go to get from here to the future. It will draw on the vast amount of detailed information gleaned from the brand healthcheck and use this to help you and your management team understand what is needed to get all your staff on brand and help them stay there. It will show you what you must do and how those responsible for the brand can develop its potential and drive it forward by creating better content, communications and experiences for your customers. You may still need to make guesses at future revenue and profit figures, but they will not tell you what your company needs to be doing today, tomorrow and in three months' time. The brand blueprint will.

I've already made the point that your brand is built from the inside out. All the stuff that shows on the outside – the salesman's attitude, the tactical ad campaigns, the personalised communications, the social media activities and engagement and all the other work that goes into building the organisation's reputation – has to come from a set of principles, ideas, beliefs and goals that are held and recognised internally.

So the brand blueprint needs to be divided into two sections – internal and external – and to pay full attention to both of them. It also needs to be broken down further into its strategic and tactical aspects, so that you can use the information and insights acquired in the brand healthcheck to start identifying the strategic and tactical objectives for your internal and external branding activities. The strategic goals embody the big picture view of where the brand is going, while the tactics will be what needs to be done to get there.

There's nothing really new here, I know, but it's amazing how many firms start with the tactics – or worse, think that strategy is just a question of stringing together a series of tactical moves.

I'm not going to start offering a bunch of generic recommendations at this point, because every company and every industry is different. It simply isn't possible to write a strategic plan for your brand without knowing the results of the healthcheck. But once the results are in, you will have a firm basis on which to build. Depending on your industry, the size and age of your company, and the opportunities identified in the brand healthcheck, you may develop anything from two to five key strategies. There will then be a number of tactics – maybe five to ten – that can be employed to move the business towards each of these strategic goals.

The internal section of the brand blueprint must define what needs to be done to align the organisation around the brand vision and its mission and values. These are the glue that holds the brand together, and everyone within the organisation must be aware of them and their importance. People need to know how their actions relate to the vision, mission and values and understand the importance of not doing anything that may conflict with them.

Without a proper brand blueprint, these can often be overlooked or forgotten. Even with a blueprint in place, though, it is not always easy. Aligning the organisation around the brand involves subtle, longer-term activities like building a customer-focused corporate culture, communicating the company's values to staff and making sure individuals incorporate the brand values into their routines.

The brand blueprint's internal section will emphasise the way the departments critical to the success of the brand – including sales, marketing, product development, accounts, logistics and, of course, your new social media department, headed by the community manager – must work together to build a coherent brand narrative. This may involve radical changes in internal thinking and processes, and it will need to be backed up with practical examples and advice on how the various departments can collaborate more effectively. The blueprint will also outline what new kinds of training and tools will be needed to ensure that all the individuals within the organisation are consistently on brand.

Externally, the brand blueprint maps out how you are going to shape the brand's personality and its relationships with customers and prospects. The focus must always be on what is best for consumers and on delivering economic, experiential and emotional value to them on their own terms. What you mustn't do is try to thrust a dull, corporate message at today's more knowledgeable, jaded and spoilt-for-choice consumers. One of the reasons this book doesn't focus on traditional marketing's obsession with identity, positioning, reach and awareness is because these things are simply too costly and time-consuming, as well as being irrelevant to most 21st-century consumers. These days, people are far more likely to discover a brand through an internet search or after discussions with friends or in a Facebook group than to be made aware of it through a TV commercial or full page advertisement in a national newspaper.

One of the main reasons for having a detailed brand blueprint is to make sure your organisation stays on brand, knows its customers, puts them first and delivers real value to them – on their terms.

Equally importantly, though, the blueprint actually *reduces* the amount of micromanaging that's needed to make all this happen. By providing a clear framework within which middle managers and front-line staff can take their own decisions and act on their own initiative, it allows the business, and the brand, to be more quick and responsive in meeting customers' needs.

This decentralised decision-making is a key factor in building a modern brand, and it can lead directly to opportunities to reach new customer segments via social media. I was thinking about this recently when I took my daughters with me on a business trip to Japan.

We were eating the same all-in set breakfast in the hotel for the fourth day running, and my kids' eyes widened with greed as they watched an appetising pile of pancakes being carried past to another table.

'Can we have pancakes, too, Dad?' my eldest daughter asked.

'I don't know. You'll have to ask them,' I said.

So my daughter asked, and was told, politely but firmly, that the pancakes were not offered as part of the all-in breakfast menu. She was disappointed, but took it well enough. And both children were amazed and delighted, a few minutes later, when a smiling waiter appeared with a generous pile of fresh pancakes, compliments of the management.

At this moment, a tiny, inexpensive local initiative, obviously unsanctioned by any top-level managers, had won this famous Japanese-owned 5-star hotel enormous kudos within my family. Indeed, both girls were still telling strangers about it in the lift several days later. The word-of-mouth ripples obviously spread a little way, but when I thought about it, I realised that the hotel had missed a trick by not asking my kids to tell the pancake story on their Facebook and Instagram pages. If the idea had just been put into their heads, I'm quite sure they would gladly have shared their happiness on Facebook, Instagrammed the pictures they took of the glistening, golden pancakes and tweeted all kinds of positive comments.

That would have given the hotel a great, heart-warming tale that would surely have been picked up and shared across all kinds of social media platforms – a little real-life story of personalised service that would have had ten times the credibility and impact of any dull, corporate ad campaign. And it would all have come from a spontaneous act of kindness by front-line staff who were either given the freedom to make their own decisions on the fly or happy to break the rules and respond to their customers in a quick and generous way.

Our experience in Japan is a classic example of the kind of decentralised decision-making and personalised attention to detail that creates genuine differentiation and helps to build a real, believable brand narrative. There was a good little story here that could have been shared across the ecosystem and potentially taken up by the mass media too.

But most brand healthchecks don't reveal much evidence of this sort of spontaneous customer service.

Far more often, they highlight the fact that organisations are using the type of old-fashioned, over-centralised, command-and-control management model that stifles initiative and condemns the brand to die a slow, painful death. This is a particular problem in SE Asia, where business owners have a reputation for being hierarchical, inflexible and reluctant to change and adopt technology, and less than keen to give even trusted employees the autonomy to make anything more than simple, routine decisions.

If your brand is to survive and thrive in the customer economy, it will be essential for you to relinquish control of certain customer-facing elements of your brand engagement. This can be difficult for many CEOs, especially those who have founded a business and seen it grow from a corner shop or a back-street factory to a publicly listed company. But it is a move that must be made.

The brand blueprint has an important role to play here. It can help the CEO step back and relinquish many of the more detailed tasks of day-to-day management, while still retaining control. Crucially it allows him to track what managers and others are doing and provides checks and balances for what managers are telling him – which may often be quite different from the reality.

One client we worked with is a fairly typical Chinese family company. Though it is now listed on the stock exchange, its chairman is still the grandfather who originally came to

Malaysia from China sixty years ago. As often happens, the grandchildren were sent to university in Australia and the UK to learn modern management skills. This made good sense, especially as the company was steadily losing market share in the face of increasingly fierce competition from local and foreign firms. But, of course, when they came back with their new-fangled ideas, the grandfather decided nothing was broken (well, nothing, at least, that couldn't be tackled by offering price discounts) so nothing needed to be fixed.

When I first met the chairman, he was still sceptical about the value of the MBAs the younger family members had brought back from the West.

'They think they know everything now,' the old man told me, speaking in Mandarin with his daughter as his interpreter. 'But they don't know how to run a business like this.'

'It's all about people and prices, and they can't teach you that at business school. As far as I'm concerned, the important part of their business education starts now.'

But he was not completely inflexible, and his attitude had softened over time. He had gradually been persuaded that the falling sales figures might be to do with being out of step with today's consumers and that it would be worth making a relatively small investment to get a detailed picture of the company's current strengths and weaknesses.

It had taken the new MBA-educated generation several years to convince the grandfather that it was time for a change. When he relented, the comprehensive brand healthcheck that followed identified multiple problems related to products, packaging, distribution, communications, customer service, staff attitudes and more. Crucially, it gave the new generation the unbiased third-party endorsements they needed to support their argument for a new approach to building for the future.

Based on the healthcheck findings, a brand blueprint was created with a completely new strategic and tactical direction and clear timelines for major changes to packaging and communications, content creation and training, alongside improvements in many key processes and systems. Budgets were allocated for previously neglected channels like Facebook and Twitter and for new technology to help the company track and communicate with customers.

The brand healthcheck and the development of the brand blueprint proved to be a genuine turning point – a coming of age for the company that set it back on track for continuing success in the modern era. The brand's history and heritage were preserved and honoured, but it quickly began to build a much closer two-way relationship with its customers, taking full advantage of the new technologies and media the younger members of the family had been trained to exploit.

There was a new energy and purpose about everything it did, and even the grandfather who had founded the company soon recognised that a profound and necessary revolution had taken place. It became a great place to work, morale improved and the long-term decline in sales was reversed as a new generation of consumers fell in love with the brand.

'The one differentiator that makes all the difference today is the relationship you have with your customers.

Getting that right means investing in new tools and technologies to bring you closer to your customers, improve your processes and add structure to your front-line operations'

CHAPTER 22

Focusing on the Front Line

My experience of working with companies in Asia and the Middle East over the past 28 years has shown that many of them are missing out on serious profits that could easily be captured by making relatively small changes.

'What is the single most significant innovation I could make this year?' one of my Malaysian friends asked me, as we celebrated Hari Raya in July 2015.

'That's easy,' I said. 'Just find a way of measuring your sales operation against the best in the world and identifying what they're doing that you're not. For example, I hardly know a company in this country with a properly structured sales department.'

'Ah,' he said. 'That's only because in a tiger economy, where demand is greater than supply, you don't need a sophisticated sales operation. You just need people to take the orders.'

'And is that what it feels like now?' I asked.

He paused.

'No,' he said. 'It doesn't. I think the way we do business is changing.'

'Then you'll have to change with it,' I said, as we tucked into yet another plateful of *ayam percik* and *lemang*.

My friend was right. The way we do business has changed. Asian firms need to up their game and make sure they have the right tools to compete in our increasingly internationalised, borderless economies. But these things are not impossibly complicated or expensive. If you recruit the right people and train them properly, and pick the right tools and use them wisely, the changes you need to make should pay for themselves in weeks or months, rather than years.

The fact is, your sales department is still the front line. It may well be the first place a consumer experiences your brand, and you've only ever got a few seconds to make the right impression. Get it wrong and you'll always be playing catch-up.

It's essential to recognise that the whole business of selling has changed enormously. Customers no longer need to see sales reps to get information on products or services. They can learn more about an industry or service in a few minutes online than they ever would by talking to a sales rep. The internet gives potential buyers direct access to consumers and businesses with similar problems to their own. They can evaluate the solutions those consumers used and get advice on the best approach long before they have any contact with your sales people. The product brochure is essentially irrelevant, and the corporate website, with its too-perfect pictures and lofty promises, cannot compete with the industry forums. Hoary old selling techniques like the sales spiel and the alternative close are buried in the sales graveyard.

The one differentiator that makes all the difference today is the relationship you have with your customers. And getting that right means investing in new tools and technologies to bring you closer to your customers, improve your processes and add structure to your front-line operations.

For one well-known property developer, taking an objective and unflinching look at every aspect of the sales process has made it possible to save on advertising budgets and still make more sales more quickly. Simply recognising that it did not have enough information about its customers and building a proper client database was a major breakthrough. Paying attention to the front line has produced spectacular payoffs.

This company had traditionally taken the short-sighted view that it only needed to hire sales people when a development project was ready to sell. The new sales team had to start from scratch every time, because the staff who had been selling the previous project had kept no useful records of their contacts with customers. People who had shown an interest but not gone on to buy the company's investment properties from one development were bound to be some of the hottest prospects for its next development project, yet there was no database of information about them that could be carried forward from year to year. When this problem was highlighted in a thorough review of the sales process, the developer introduced a third-party customer relationship management system for the first time, with dramatic and immediately profitable results.

Another Fusionbrand client, a general insurance broker in Kuala Lumpur that works closely with Lloyds of London, was able to increase its share of wallet among 30 per cent of its existing customers as a direct result of changes prompted by a sales process review.

In this case, the review revealed that an inexperienced sales manager, promoted to this key position because he was an old and trusted friend of the CEO, needed advice and help to develop a more professional sales operation. By improving training, motivation and reporting, with a clear and straightforward sales manual to guide new and existing staff, the sales manager was able to transform his team's performance. Staff turnover came down, more prospects were seen and many more first-time sales were made.

Perhaps even more significantly, there were far more meetings with existing customers, which led to deeper, longer and more profitable relationships.

This isn't rocket science. But it is incredible how many companies in Asia that were continuously profitable through the tiger economy days of the 1990s and 2000s ignored the basics of business in the rush for sales. They ignored the changing environment and the arrival of new technologies, too – and that has left them ill equipped to deal with today's tougher and increasingly international competition. Understandably, even those that recognise the need for change find it hard to know when and how to start.

'When?' is the easy question, because the answer just has to be 'Now.'

'How?' is more difficult, because it depends on the exact circumstances each company finds itself in.

A full-scale brand healthcheck may raise major strategic issues that demand a lot of thought and planning. But a thorough sales process review invariably highlights a shortlist of priorities that can be tackled immediately to produce immediate improvements in performance. It's not a quick fix for every problem, but it does offer the chance to make vital changes and adjustments that will have a direct impact on front-line interactions with prospects and customers.

The sales process review methodology Fusionbrand has developed over the years is robust and disciplined. It is all about providing benchmarks and ideas for improvements that will lead directly to a leaner organisation, more satisfied and loyal customers and a healthy, durable and profitable brand.

Though the company involved has to be ready to look at itself objectively, the investment needed is modest. And the paybacks can be quick and substantial. A comprehensive sales process review can deliver a clutch of valuable business benefits, including enhancing prospect identification and sales personnel performance, indicating which tools are working and which aren't, improving closing rates and providing a sustainable boost to revenue.

The review project has to start with the basics. It must begin by identifying all the key players, from the company's management and sales force to the people who buy the product, and determining what each of these groups requires from the sales process. Eventually, it will need to incorporate input from external customers and suppliers, managers, marketing and sales personnel, and people in several other parts of the organisation as well.

But the first step is always to look at the situation as it is – key factors such as the suitability of the personnel involved and how leads are generated and processed – and to trace the sequence of events to uncover what happens to each lead as it progresses towards a sale or some other outcome.

Of course, even that may reveal unexpected weaknesses. We worked with a digital media company that had been struggling along with no proper lead management processes and no lead progress tracking. Despite being in a cutting edge industry, this company was frustratingly traditional in its approach. Sales people always seemed to be selling features, rather than benefits, and they were often reluctant to ask key questions in case they somehow offended their prospects.

'How do you expect to make a sale if you know so little about the person you are selling to?' I asked one employee, during a confidential interview.

'Oh, I'd love to know more, but people here would see that as invading their privacy,' he said. 'I cannot just ask "How much can you afford to spend on digital screens?" without putting the prospect off.'

Some people will say that's a cultural issue. But it's not about the difference between Asian and European cultures. It's purely a matter of technique. You can't ask questions as crude as that and expect to get a good reception in New York or London, any more than you can in KL, Singapore or Bangkok. Knowing what questions to ask and how to ask them in ways that will give you the information you need without scaring off the customer is something that can be addressed in industry-specific training sessions, in sales guidelines and in your sales manual.

The front line review also involves a thorough analysis of the company's sales tools and processes. It looks at all the key elements, from the way data is collected and processed to lead handling, sales cycles, prospect, customer and inter-organisational engagement, post-sale procedures and other operational and measurement issues. It examines data collection and reporting requirements, reviews the forms and other documents that are used and looks in detail at process steps and timetables.

But sales organisations are not all about data and processes. As everyone knows, individuals have their own strengths and weaknesses.

Good sales people may be sociable, curious and energetic, or they may be analytical, meticulous and less keen on face-to-face meetings with customers. Both approaches can be effective, and a great team will usually need a mix of personality types. Part of the overall sales process must be concerned with developing ways of sharing intelligence, learning and experience to improve results. So the sales process review puts the sales team under the microscope, too, assessing the quality and range of people's selling skills, product knowledge, cross- and up-selling capabilities, personal responsiveness and operational efficiency.

Inevitably, some sales staff will fall short of the mark, either through lack of training and experience or because they find it hard to identify with customers' needs. I remember going for a test drive in a new Lexus recently and meeting just such a person. When I arrived at the showroom, the woman who greeted me could not have been less engaging.

'This is the car. It comes in three colours and costs so

much,' she said, or words to that effect. Not a good start, I felt, but I let it go and we set off for the test drive.

The car impressed me, and I loved some of the advanced gadgetry the manufacturer had come up with. I was starting to get quite interested. Back at the showroom, I was playing with the navigation system when the woman physically took my hand off the control and proceeded to show me how it worked. She obviously had no idea of the value to me of experiencing the system for myself. I was shocked – not so much that she had moved my hand away, but that anyone working in auto sales today should fail to understand the buyer's need to touch, feel and smell the vehicle, as well as looking at it and collecting factual information.

Even if this sales person did not see the world the way I did, I knew she could have been trained not to alienate a potential buyer in such an obvious way.

She didn't need to be a naturally warm, extrovert personality. She just needed to be told, as a matter of technique, that she would win more sales if she was more responsive to what aspects of the car the individual prospect needed to experience directly. I was there in my own right as a potential customer, but if I had been working on a sales process review for Lexus, I would immediately have made a note that this was an area where a little relationship training would go a lot further than yet more product training days.

Away from the specific issue of customer responsiveness, the review exercise will analyse sales processes, workflows and practices – including lead handling and management, closing rates, territory development, sales competency and quotas – to find out if the people who are tasked with representing your brand to the world are engaging consumers effectively.

The aim is not to make a sale, but to make and keep a customer, as legendary management guru Peter Drucker always emphasised. After all, it is positive experience with your business that turns a one-off customer into a continuing source of profitable income and a brand ambassador, which in turn builds your brand.

I have run sales process reviews like this for companies in many different sectors in Europe, the Middle East and Asia, and the results are usually surprising and always beneficial.

Impartial analysis of all the factors mentioned so far invariably generates valuable insights that were not apparent to those on the inside. This probably shouldn't be unexpected. Informed objectivity is always hard to achieve, and it is particularly hard for people involved in the day-to-day running of a sales operation to stand back and analyse the situation from an outsider's perspective.

The other major element of these projects is even harder for insiders to replicate. Any comprehensive sales process review needs to go beyond looking at numbers and procedures and get to grips with the human interactions involved.

The key to this is a programme of confidential interviews and on-the-spot observations in which the candid and sometimes off-the-cuff comments of sales staff, senior management, customers and prospects can reveal all kinds of new opportunities. If time and resources allow, there should also be interviews with people from departments like finance and new product development that interact with the sales department. In today's social economy, it is not just the sales team that affects front-line performance.

As well as asking people what they do and how they do it, the analyst will want to watch what actually happens during prospecting, selling and closing activities, both face to face and on the telephone. Experience teaches that what is observed does not always tally with what people say they are doing, and this may lead to action to correct weaknesses or to define best practices that can be rolled out to improve performance across the front-line team.

The results of all this research can be startling – and sometimes disturbing. But even if the news looks bad, this is information you need to know, as the first step towards putting things right. By identifying outdated or ineffective processes, weaknesses in data collection or lead handling and poor follow-through with prospects and customers, the sales process review can pay for itself many times over.

It's true, of course, that the short-term gains will not always be as clear cut as those enjoyed by the insurance broker I mentioned earlier. But just putting in place a well-thought-out and realistic sales manual – whether it's ten pages long or a hundred – will help management as well as staff and drive the sales department forward.

The positive results generally include lower recruitment costs, better staff retention, stronger sales management and a better focused, trained, organised and motivated sales force, plus the kind of close relationships with customers that lead to a lifetime of sales.

Once the results of the sales process review are documented in a manual that standardises processes and customer interactions, optimises the use of the CRM system and sets performance benchmarks that include retention as a key indicator, sales managers find they can focus more of their time on the more important and creative aspects of the job.

Routine tasks become less onerous, training is quicker and more effective and lower sales force turnover means overall productivity is improved. As the enhanced processes in the new sales manual are incorporated into the team's short- and long-term selling activities, predictable payoffs include increased volume, with a shorter selling cycle and a lower cost of sales, improved retention rates and higher levels of engagement with customers, leading to deeper, more durable relationships and spontaneous recommendations and referrals.

These are all major business benefits, but they are

particularly important for local companies threatened by the current flood of powerful and well funded international competitors.

Asian firms must learn to play to their strengths and use every bit of local knowledge they can lay their hands on to fight back against the invaders. Thanks to the development of the internet, there are plenty of opportunities to do this now in ways that were not possible even ten years ago.

But your international competition didn't get big by accident. To win this kind of battle, you will need to be at your best. The winners will be those companies that are smarter, leaner, more efficient and able to make the most of their resources to build better customer relationships and sell more effectively. Commissioning a sales process review to help you fine tune the performance of all your front-line staff is the first step towards securing your company's future.

'These days you get the customer response you deserve.

Branding is no longer a matter of what you say; it's all about what you do'

CHAPTER 23

Implementing the Brand Blueprint

When we look at all the examples of firms that have spent billions of dollars on advertising and seen their market share plummet, sales go through the floor and profits disappear, it's obvious that something has to change. If McDonalds can spend US$6 billion on advertising over five years, only to see its profits slump by 30% in 2014, what hope is there for companies that don't have enormous budgets to spend and that can't afford to take that kind of hit?

McDonalds has made some huge one-off mistakes, such as its attempt, a couple of years ago, to introduce deep fried chicken wings as a major new offering in all its 14,000 US outlets. The launch was accompanied by a massive eight-week advertising campaign, but people just didn't like the product. The project tanked – and McDonalds was left licking its wounds and trying to work out what to do with an embarrassing pile of 4,500 tonnes of unwanted chicken wings.

But that's not why the fast food giant's profits are down. It's not the occasional spectacular cock-up that's causing the problem. It's the fact that health-conscious consumers are turning away from burgers, buns and fries. It's the cumulative effect of many negative headlines – about poor food quality, low pay and bad treatment of workers. It's because McDonalds has confused purchase frequency with loyalty. It's because it has continued to focus on low-priced commodity products that increasingly affluent and health-conscious consumers are often keen to leave behind. And it's because it has relied far too much on hip slogans and heavyweight advertising campaigns to keep people coming through the doors and to try to reach the next generation of potential customers. Now it faces a problem that advertising can't solve, and it doesn't know how to handle it. Even bringing in a new CEO in March 2015 failed to stop the slide, which continued with a 13% fall in profits in the second quarter of the year.

If big-budget mass media advertising no longer works for McDonalds, what hope is there for the rest of us? If McDonalds can't make it work with US$6 billion, how far are you going to get with US$6 million or US$600,000? There has to be a better way to build tomorrow's brands than trying to shout louder than the giants who can afford to spend – and even waste – billions.

As I've said throughout this book, I'm not anti-advertising. For many companies, in many situations, a certain amount of advertising is always going to be a necessary part of the drive to acquire customers. But it should only ever be a small tactical part of your brand strategy, never the driving force – and it certainly can't be relied on to build your brand.

One-size-fits-all campaigns pumped out across the mass media simply won't work any more. You can't expect a young, upwardly-mobile banker in Jakarta and a single mother of five in central Thailand to respond to the same message. Yet many brands try to market themselves in exactly the same way across all the countries of SE Asia, keeping the same slogans and commercials and simply dubbing them into our local languages. It's not working now, and it will work even worse in the next few years. You can shout as loud as you like, but people will not be persuaded.

Instead of trying to shout louder than everyone else,

companies need to talk to consumers and develop conversations with their customers, treating them as real people and listening to their voices. The dynamics of marketing have changed. The most powerful brand-building tool today is still the voice of the consumer. But now that voice is amplified. And that voice can now be heard, outspoken and unfiltered, every day of the year, on social media – on Facebook, Instagram and Twitter – where consumers connect directly with each other. We live in a world where everyone has a say. Consumers can describe and share their experiences and opinions, instantly and at no cost, and their views can be repeated and amplified on an unprecedented scale by their friends and followers.

We all know how it works in practice in our own lives.

Maybe I like the look of a BMW X3. Needless to say, the BMW website will tell me it's great. The downloadable brochure will tell me it's great and of course the sales rep in the showroom will tell me it's great. Until recently, those were my only sources of information, except for possible mentions in the press. And, to be honest, few publications were prepared to print anything that would upset their major advertisers and potentially lose them revenue.

These days, though, I can go online and learn from and engage people who have actually bought an X3. And if I find that owners are saying the acceleration and fuel consumption are not nearly as good as the brand's website tells me or the service at my nearest dealer is not up to scratch, I can make up my own mind. I can decide whether or not to choose this car in the light of the experiences of those who have actually bought one. And if those experiences are broadly negative, no amount of advertising is likely to make me ignore the warning signs.

There is no better selling tool than an unsolicited recommendation. There is something uniquely powerful about the emotional honesty, the trust and credibility that a heartfelt Facebook post or tweet can generate – something no print ad or TV commercial can hope to match. But we've all seen the way complaints about outrageously bad treatment of customers can go viral. Some of the most popular posts of all are those where disgruntled customers complain – often with bitter and engaging humour – about the bad treatment or poor products they've received from big companies.

These are the messages that stick, and they are no longer under the control of the corporate marketers. These days you get the customer response you deserve. Branding is no longer a matter of what you say; it's all about what you do.

One famous example of how doing the right thing translates into powerful branding involved Morton's, one of New York's favourite chains of steakhouse restaurants, and US marketing and investment guru Peter Shankman.

Shankman, a Twitter enthusiast since 2007, has 170,000 followers. Based on earlier tweets, Morton's on-the-ball social media team had already been tracking him as a regular visitor and a potentially influential fan. So when Shankman found himself stuck in the airport in Tampa, Florida, on his way to New York and idly tweeted that he was dying to sink his teeth into a Morton's steak, the company spotted an opportunity and sprang into action. The steakhouse found out which flight he was on and arranged for him to be surprised at the airport by a tuxedo-clad waiter from the nearest branch, at Hackensack, 40km from Newark. As he walked out into Arrivals, he was presented with a Morton's bag containing a medium-rare 24oz Porterhouse steak and various other goodies.

Shankman was tickled pink and duly reported the whole delightful experience on his blog, attracting 250 comments and leading to 7,000 shares on Twitter, as people gasped at this extraordinary level of fast, responsive customer service. The story was eventually picked up by CBS News, the *Huffington Post* and even the *Daily Mail* in London, being seen by millions of people. I don't know whether the enterprising social media guys who pulled off this stunt got a big bonus for their work, but they certainly deserved one. The huge, viral wave of positive publicity must have been worth millions to Morton's.

And it proved a hugely important point. As Peter Shankman himself said afterwards: 'Customer service is no longer about telling people how great you are. It's about producing amazing moments in time, and letting those moments become the focal point of how amazing you are, told not by you, but by the customer who you thrilled.'

Both the action of ambushing Shankman with the steak his heart desired and the speed of response that made it possible were important here.

In this new environment, brands can't prosper just by being in the right place at the right time. They have to be in the right place *all* the time. They can't control the message, so they need to build dialogue and conversations with their consumers. They can't push out a corporate slogan and expect it to change perceptions. Instead of pushing, they need to pull customers in by adopting a communication strategy based on information, engagement and added value.

So how can you do this? How do you begin to implement a branding strategy that goes beyond the limitations of mass market advertising?

One important element is the use of branded content. Branded content aims to marry the influence, trust and credibility of editorial comment with the messaging reach of advertising and direct marketing. The key is to give the consumer something of value, whether it's information, education, or just a smile to brighten up the day.

It's not a new idea. We've all seen the traditional examples, such as advertorials, white papers and guest columns in the press and online. But today's branded content ranges from free e-books (complete with contact details for future relationship building) and digital magazines to blogs, Facebook pages and applications and messages sent via Twitter, Snapchat, Line, Whatsapp, Instagram and many other platforms.

Video, often in the form of clips created spontaneously on smartphones by customers and consumers, has emerged as a core element of branded content. When Lego stepped in to help a disappointed 11-year-old boy with Asperger's Syndrome find the discontinued Emerald Night Train set he'd been saving up for – sending it to him free of charge as a surprise birthday present – the Danish company's goodhearted initiative was rewarded with 2 million views of the YouTube video of the ecstatic young fan opening the parcel.

Simply providing a platform that encourages consumers to engage with aspects of the brand can help create positive perceptions. Malaysia Airlines, for instance, which has made so many branding mistakes in the past, has started encouraging travellers to post their own photos of its planes on Facebook, as a step towards building community engagement. It's a tiny step, but branding is about tiny steps – and, for once, it is a step in the right direction.

There are so many opportunities to get people thinking and talking about your brand, but they all depend on providing something your audience will value. For one financial services company in Singapore, the breakthrough was launching a robust, energetic e-newsletter that talks about money with a blunt honesty people have not met before. This straight-talking approach has won it lots of new friends, expanding its reach in all kinds of unexpected directions as subscribers have rushed to share the newsletter online with colleagues and business contacts.

A regional furniture brand with a factory in the Philippines and outlets across SE Asia has used its specialist knowledge of furniture care to boost its search engine rankings. By offering practical advice and inviting consumers to comment, share their experiences and add their own hints and tips, it has built up a substantial online community and a lively flow of conversation that is doing wonders for its profile and credibility. This is the best kind of branded content, a rich mix of company-sponsored advice and consumer-generated discussion that will both consolidate the brand in its home markets and – because the internet knows no borders – start to create a brand personality in other countries that may eventually be targets for future expansion.

Part of the art of using branded content is recognising where and when it can be repurposed for use in other situations. If you have commissioned how-to articles, for example, these can form the basis of blog posts and conference presentations, while paragraphs of advice and readers' tips can be lifted for use as comments in forums and discussion groups. Developing a wide range of branded content gives your company a stock of material that can be used time and again, in many different contexts across different social media platforms.

But generating and exploiting branded content is only part of the story. You need to identify all the gaps in your brand and understand what you need to do to make sure your staff members are all behaving in line with the brand personality. You need to make certain your company is ready and able to deliver on the promises it makes and that your marketing collateral, formal and informal, physical and digital, is right for the people you want to talk to. And you need to develop a brand plan that will guide you along the right track.

I'm not saying any of this is easy. But now the brand blueprint has set out what you need to do, you are ready to take the steps needed to acquire and retain the customers who will work with you to build your brand.

Just in case you are still not convinced, let me remind you

of something I mentioned earlier – the simple fact that 80% of purchases are repeat purchases.

Overwhelmingly, the people who buy a product are the people who bought it before, and the time before that. It's a sobering thought. That means all the traditional advertising we see is actually aimed at convincing the floating voters – that 20% minority of people who haven't already made up their minds to buy their usual brand.

A mass media advertising campaign is going to have to be pretty good to convince them, assuming, of course, it is even able to cut through all the clutter and competitive noise. And how convincing is it ever likely to be, compared with a spontaneous, heartfelt recommendation seen on social media? Don't you think those undecided buyers are more likely to be persuaded by a recommendation shared by a friend or by a comment from a likeminded person on social media than by the hectoring of a press ad or a billboard?

When it comes to launching a new product and taking the first steps towards building a brand, it's important to understand how the take-up of new ideas and products really works. There has been a lot of research on this topic, and the results are remarkably consistent. Whenever a new product, technology or technique is first introduced, the way it is taken up and spread invariably follows a classic pattern, known to the theorists as the S-curve model for the diffusion of innovation.

Initially, few people will know about it. These pioneers, the innovators, have a hunger and a curiosity for new ideas that drives them to take a chance on untried products and technologies. They are the ones who will pick up the online buzz about the next big thing – and they have to be first to try it out.

They are the people queuing at midnight outside the Apple store for the latest iPad, test-driving the new Audi on the day it is launched or crowding into the big-screen cinema for the first showing of the long-awaited Star Wars movie. They'd rather have a new app in beta form now – even if there are a few glitches that still need to be ironed out – than wait six months for a bug-free version. They have high expectations and they'll be quick to let the world know if they are disappointed. But if you can get them on your side, these influential pioneers will be powerful allies in getting your message out to the world.

After the innovators come the early adopters. They are keen, but cautious. They are not going to dive in until they've heard the verdict of the critics and media commentators and seen what comments are posted by the innovation junkies and industry bloggers. They wouldn't touch an untried beta test version of your new software with a ten-foot bargepole. But as soon as they see evidence that the new arrival is offering something substantially better than what they have already, they will be eager to get their hands on it.

There are a lot more early adopters than innovators in the world, and they are the key to spreading the good word about your new product or service.

They will talk about it face to face, in their conversations with friends and business contacts. More importantly, though, they will tell their online friends – a much bigger group that will often number hundreds or thousands. Using blogs and tweets, Facebook pages and forum comments, they will pass on the excitement and build the buzz. By the time they've had their say, news of your product or service will have got out to just as many people as you might ever hope to reach with the one-way messaging of a mass media ad campaign. The difference is, of course, that these people are likely to have things in common with the early adopters who've told them about it, so the take-up rate is always going to be higher. And they will believe what the early adopters tell them a lot more readily than they accept the claims you make in a paid advertisement.

In the past, the early adopters usually learned of the

existence of a new product via a company's mass market advertising campaigns. Today, these campaigns are often irrelevant. Even when they're not, they are viewed with a scepticism few advertisers want to admit to.

These days, if early adopters aren't already on the company's mailing list (and they should be), social media and online news and technology sites are likely to be the source of most of their information. That's why it's so important, in implementing your brand blueprint, to be sure you make the most of the key influencers – digital journalists and pundits, bloggers, active tweeters, LinkedIn groups and people, consumers and professionals, who contribute to forums and comparison sites.

Many, perhaps most, new offerings fail at the early adopter stage. But if you can get these people on your side, you've practically got it made. In today's hyperconnected world, they are the key to making the next step and reaching the mainstream majority. As the sales graphs begin to climb and you start gearing up to meet the accelerating demand, you can congratulate yourself on having achieved a successful launch and laid the foundations for a winning brand

The final stage of the diffusion of innovation S-curve is the smaller group of buyers known as the laggards. Sales growth begins to flatten off again once the needs of the mainstream majority have been satisfied, forming the top of the S and leaving you with a mature product that can only be sold to the diehards who are most resistant to change. We all know people who are still sticking to Yahoo! for their email or doggedly resisting the appeal of smartphones and insisting on using simple 2005-style candybar mobiles. Innovation holds no charm for these laggards. They are interested in reliability, above all else, and their ideal guarantee of reliability is the knowledge that a product has been around for years and been used by millions of people.

The challenges involved in managing mainstream successes or mature products that are approaching obsolescence are not negligible, but we don't need to go into them here. My readers, like my clients, are much more likely to be facing the challenges of launching new products and creating brand momentum than grappling with the task of wringing the last few dollars out of an end-of-life product that has already enjoyed its time in the sun.

Looking at the way the S-curve should inform your implementation of the brand blueprint, it is clear that the early adopters are the key. You must start by identifying and priming the innovators, but it is how well you handle the early adopters that will be the make-or-break factor. Unless you've been keeping a close eye on developments in your area, you will almost certainly have been underestimating the sheer reach of social media comment.

It's obvious that a site like TripAdvisor, with its 350 million unique monthly visitors and 300 million reviews, is vitally important to the travel trade, and to travellers themselves. But more specialised sites and forums can be hugely influential, too. For example, a key site for carriers and passengers these days is FlyerTalk, which bills itself as the world's most popular frequent flyer community and is also used by a lot of airline cabin crew. FlyerTalk's numbers are piffling compared with TripAdvisor, but the level of debate and detailed information is impressive and it does have 620,000 members, including plenty of enthusiastic chatterboxes with 10,000 or more posts to their names. FlyerTalk often has 7,000 active users online at a particular moment.

On a more homely level, Mumsnet, the UK parenting site, boasts 220,000 online followers, a Bloggers Network with over 5,000 registered bloggers and 70 million page views per month. Its campaigning rival, Netmums, claims 1.9 million members and 8 million visitors a month. And so it goes on. In every market and every sphere of interest, there are communities that can reach huge and genuinely self-selecting audiences, providing a real alternative to the hit-and-hope tactics of mass media advertising.

These are big numbers. And, if you can create a presence in the right communities, they are big numbers made up of individuals who are potentially interested in your brand. You won't need to spend huge amounts of money shouting to make yourself heard, because these are people who will be happy to listen if you have something relevant for them and you say it in the right place.

Instead of relying on brute force and expensive advertising campaigns to try and attract customers and build a brand, you need to do three things, all of which should be clearly outlined in your brand blueprint.

The first is to build up a database of friends, fans, posters, followers, bloggers, prospects, influencers, advocates and customers and get to know them so that you can tailor your promotions to their particular needs.

The second is to create interesting, useful branded content and use your constantly growing database to help you share and spread it across the digital universe. As you create and share the content you know your followers, friends and customers want, encourage interactions and shared conversations and work at keeping the brand narrative moving, you will create a momentum that ensures your brand has a life of its own. As the web of conversations widens and consumer talks to consumer, your brand will even grow while you sleep.

This kind of quiet, careful, cumulative brand building is nowhere near as exciting as having a bright young team of beautiful creative agency people telling you how wonderful you are (though you can still have that in connection with the odd tactical campaign). But if you are really serious about building a brand, rather than just seeing your name on a billboard, you need to be looking at collecting the right data. This is the key to building personalised relationships with your customers, so that you can be sure the content you provide is what they want to receive.

British Airways, which flies direct from the UK to Singapore and Bangkok and resumed its services into Kuala Lumpur in 2015, is one global company that knows more than most about its customers. It is assiduous in collecting all the relevant information it can get about its passengers to allow it to deliver a personalised, seamless and largely stress-free travel experience. BA knows this is the key to building and sustaining a successful global brand – so much so that it took the unusual step, in 2015, of setting up a specialised customer experience unit.

If you are flying BA from London to Kuala Lumpur, Bangkok or Singapore, the carrier will ask you once for your passport details and then store that data securely. As the airline gets to know you, it will collect information about how you like to travel to Heathrow (and sometimes even arrange parking at a preferential rate). It will keep track of which ticket classes you choose, where you like to sit and what kind of in-flight meals you prefer. If you fly frequently, you will be welcomed personally on arrival at the airport. Like most other airlines, BA will ask permission to contact you with travel offers and other special deals. Unlike many, though, it takes the trouble to make sure these are personalised and keyed to your specific likes and interests, so you are not bombarded with irritating and irrelevant emails. The devil is in the detail, and BA is exceptionally good at using the information it has collected to enhance its service to the individual customer, rather than merely trying to sell what it has to offer.

The contrast with Malaysia Airlines couldn't be more stark. When I last flew back from London to KL, in business class, I received an email from Malaysia Airlines asking for my comments and feedback on my journey. That's good, basic, routine stuff. But my heart sank as I looked at the first question: 'Which flight were you on?'

For heaven's sake. If the carrier doesn't already know which flight I took, what hope is there? How optimistic can I be that Malaysia Airlines will take note of my comments, if its systems are so unco-ordinated that it needs me to fill in the flight number?

The third thing you must do, in the light of the insights provided by the brand blueprint, is understand what your brand currently means to consumers and how the industry or market you are in is changing. This is why it is so important not to skip the auditing process that provides your brand healthcheck. Once you have a clear picture of your brand in relation to today's market realities, you will be equipped to think clearly about where you should be taking it.

Just to reiterate, the point is that branding, these days, is about relationships, rather than products.

The world's largest media company, Facebook, doesn't create any content, and the largest taxi company, Uber, doesn't use its own cars. The company with the largest inventory of rooms, Airbnb, doesn't have a single hotel and the largest financial institution, Paypal, doesn't own any banks.

The old, transactional business model, in which your ambition is to sell whatever you have to whoever you can whenever you can (and if you can't, to discount until you find your buyers), is being overtaken by wholly new business models built around relationships. Customers are looking for something different, for the unique combination of social, economic and experiential value that only a fully developed brand can consistently deliver.

The internet has changed our world and changed the rules of the game. It has placed relationships, and the brands that can make the most of them, right at the heart of business. It has opened up new opportunities for young and growing businesses that they can afford to exploit – and must exploit, if they are to make headway against the power of the international corporations. In SE Asia, a fast-growing market that's become a key expansion target for these global giants, there is no future in trying to use mass-market advertising and other outdated marketing techniques to slug it out with the big boys. They will simply crush you underfoot. But careful, intelligent implementation of a well-thought-out brand blueprint, making full use of the right data and the right social media opportunities, offers the chance to build the kind of committed, loyal and engaged customer base the mass-market dinosaurs can only dream of.

'Our recommendation was clear. By all means start negotiations with the manufacturers to see if they're prepared to change.

In the meantime, though, just scrap the ad campaigns and save these millions for use where the money can do a lot more good'

CHAPTER 24

How Tourism Malaysia Saved and Went Social

Creativity is overrated. It has its part to play in every aspect of brand building and communication, but it is not the key factor in determining success or failure.

Likeable ad campaigns, memorable slogans and stunning imagery are simply not enough to build a brand. Getting the creative work right is no longer the silver bullet that guarantees success. It probably never was, but it certainly isn't now.

Without a real understanding of who you are trying to reach, how you can reach these people, what they want and why they should choose you, any serious attempt to create a brand and build a community of loyal and enthusiastic customers is doomed to fail. That's why virtually all of Fusionbrand's work is grounded in careful, well-targeted research. But it's a lesson few organisations in Southeast Asia have taken to heart.

When we began our work for Tourism Malaysia, we quickly discovered we were working with a client that did not have convincing answers to these essential who/how/what/why questions.

The agency, funded by the Ministry of Tourism and Culture, is responsible for promoting one of the country's most important industries. Tourism is Malaysia's second biggest export earner. It was attracting well over 21 million visitors a year, generating RM50bn (US$15bn) in revenue for the country. But destination branding is a tough, *unforgiving business. Despite a massive advertising budget, the rate of growth was slowing, competition was increasing and, crucially, visitors were spending less and not coming back. Malaysia's repeat visitor rate was much lower than those of its most important regional rivals like Thailand and Singapore, and this was rightly seen as a threat to future growth.*

I remember talking about these problems to my colleagues, as we prepared our Tourism Malaysia pitch presentation.

'This isn't going to be easy,' they grumbled. 'Every country in Asia and beyond is going to be upping its marketing budget and fighting for market share. How do we know we can come up with something different enough to make Malaysia stand out?'

'I don't know the answer to that yet,' I replied. 'But I do know we won't get there by sitting around trying to dream up witty creative slogans. If we get the contract, it's going to take a lot of footslogging and research to find out what we really need to be offering visitors.'

'That sounds like hard work, Marcus,' muttered a voice from the back.

'But that's just it,' I said. 'We know what has to be done, and we've got the methodology to do it. We've never been afraid of working hard, so let's just show them why our way's the best.'

'OK,' someone grunted. 'You're the boss. I just hope you'll try to land us something a bit more straightforward next time.'

Despite the challenges, Tourism Malaysia was still an attractive prospect for any branding professional. The high profile and the lure of the agency's US$200 million advertising budget made for a very competitive pitching process. Fusionbrand only won the business after a long and hard-fought selection battle. In the end, though, the agency's managers responded positively to our data-driven, customer-centred approach and to my insistence that outdated strategies based on awareness, reach, positioning and repeated me-too tactical campaigns simply could not achieve their ambitious growth targets.

That wasn't a message they necessarily wanted to hear, but the agency was already uncomfortably aware of the diminishing returns it was getting from its traditional advertising activities.

Differentiation is tough when there is hardly a tourist destination in Asia that can't put together a convincing set of images of white, sandy beaches, turquoise waters and azure skies. With more than a thousand national and regional economic development agencies competing for attention, even the most trendy and creative ad campaigns stand little chance these days of cutting through the media clutter.

Worse still, the nature of the market has been changing rapidly, in ways that make it even harder to talk to the right people. Media fragmentation and the influence of the internet and social networks are dramatically shifting the goalposts, and the latest figures I could find, produced by the Association of British Travel Agents (ABTA), showed that two thirds of all packaged holidays were being booked online, with less than 30% of customers bothering to use travel agents.

If it hoped to get back on a strong growth path, Tourism Malaysia would need a fresh strategy, firmly based on the new realities of this changing situation. It would need accurate and up-to-date information about current attitudes and preferences and detailed data on perceptions of Malaysia among travel agents, previous visitors and those who had never visited the country.

This would lay the foundation for a new approach, based on pinpoint targeting of high-impact segments of the market and the intelligent use of digital and social media to build and nurture a powerful and engaging brand.

The agency would also need to get out of the habit of shooting itself in the foot by saying the wrong things at the wrong time.

For example, almost every piece of tourism marketing collateral it put out carried the grim warning that people convicted of drug trafficking in Malaysia could potentially be hanged. While this was important information for a very small and unwelcome minority of overseas visitors, merely mentioning it created a harsh and negative impression that was bound to affect many others who were never in any danger of falling foul of the law.

As we began to put together the elements of our research process, I thought about the huge range of audiences we would need to address.

Tourism Malaysia had specified 12 target markets. It wanted to see more visitors coming from Europe (the UK, Germany, France and Sweden) and from the US and Australia. At the same time, it was very keen to boost the number of holidaymakers from within Asia, from Indonesia, Vietnam, Korea and Japan. And it believed there was great potential in the Middle East, if free-spending visitors from Saudi Arabia and the UAE could be made aware of the excellent clothes and other bargains available in Malaysia's modern shopping malls.

So I started planning the details of our multi-market multi-level research programme. We would need to set up separate focus groups in each of the 12 target countries to collect the first-hand opinions of two key groups of potential customers – those who had been to Malaysia in the last three years and those who had travelled long-haul but never visited Malaysia – and of the local travel agents in each market.

We'd need to dig deeper with the travel industry experts in each market, too, which would involve arranging over 140 face-to-face interviews with tourism operators and agencies, journalists and local tourism associations. This would enable us to compile an external brand audit that could be set alongside our internal brand audit, itself based on 24 in-depth interviews with Tourism Malaysia staff in Kuala Lumpur and abroad.

We would also carry out an experiential audit of Tourism Malaysia branches, at home and in each of the 12 countries, to collect real-world data and observe exactly how the agency engaged with visitors. This is always an important reality check, as the results of these anonymous swoops are often very different from the accounts given by staff members.

All this intelligence-gathering work on the ground would take six months, during which time we would also be busy conducting online surveys (country by country and internationally, via the Tourism Malaysia website) and implementing a unique consumer-generated media (CGM) monitoring programme. This was a major investment, costing US$35,000 a month at that time, though these days most of *the same information can be gathered for a lot less, simply by making shrewd use of Google Alerts and Facebook Insights, or through the use of inexpensive tools such as HootSuite or Trackur.*

We were proud of this programme, as it was a huge and enlightening project, quite unlike anything any other destination marketer had undertaken before, and it involved us in scanning and analysing 22 million blogs, 60,000 usenet forums, 6,000 discussion forums and countless websites, podcasts and other social media channels. This was revolutionary. In particular, the emphasis on social media was way ahead of its time – and it's why we're a leader in this field now. By the end of it all, we could be confident we knew more about who was saying what online about travel and tourism in Malaysia than anyone else in the world.

In fact, we probably had a better all-round view of Malaysian tourism and its current place in the world than had ever been pieced together before. And our efforts led to a vast number of recommendations and insights. More than 300 specific and actionable recommendations were incorporated into a comprehensive, segment-based brand blueprint, covering everything from targets, measurements, activities and timelines to responsibilities and budgets.

It wasn't all good news, of course. In the Middle East, for example, our research uncovered one or two completely unforeseen problems.

Many visitors from the UAE and Saudi Arabia had been suitably impressed by the design and quality of the clothes on offer in Malaysia, but they had almost all returned home without buying any of this merchandise.

The problem was not that they did not want to snap up the stylish and well-made bargains that had caught their eye. It was just that the clothes they liked in the Kuala Lumpur shops were designed to fit Malaysian people – and both men's and women's clothes were always too small for the bigger build of the Middle Eastern visitors.

Unless the Malaysian garment-makers and retailers were prepared to manufacture and carry stock specifically intended for sale to overseas purchasers, the enterprising idea of targeting long-haul shoppers from Saudi Arabia and the Gulf states was simply never going to work.

Tourism Malaysia had been spending RM20 million a year (about US$7m), year in and year out, pursuing this impossible dream. In the light of the strong evidence from Fusionbrand's research that this investment would never pay off, it was clear that the whole idea was doomed to fail. No amount of advertising, however persuasive, would change that. Our recommendation was clear. By all means start negotiations with the manufacturers to see if they're prepared to change, we said. In the meantime, though, just scrap the ad campaigns and save these millions for use where the money can do a lot more good.

Another insight thrown up by our research was the different response to the 'Malaysia, Truly Asia' campaign line in different parts of the world.

In Europe and the US, it was seen as a very attractive theme. One woman in a New York focus group even startled the other participants by bursting into song and giving her own rendition of the campaign jingle. But the same campaign had gone down like a lead balloon with potential visitors in Vietnam.

'We are a proud nation with more than 4,000 years of culture and history,' one Vietnamese participant grumbled. 'There is nothing Malaysia can teach us about being "truly Asian". Like most people here, I find this slogan really offensive.'

As always, of course, it became clear that a one-size-fits-all approach to marketing Malaysia's attractions was not going to be successful.

What was needed was a coherent plan, based on the brand blueprint, that got the global organisation on brand and took advantage of the synergies to be gained from consistent messaging and presentation, but that would also customise and fine-tune the offering to match the needs of different markets. We worked with Tourism Malaysia to identify just five key target segments with the potential for strong and profitable growth and then to put in place the structures, training, metrics and online and offline messages to make that growth happen.

The brand blueprint called for a major reallocation of marketing resources, away from the previous emphasis on costly mass media campaigns and towards subtler, cheaper and more engaging approaches based largely on the intelligent use of social media, backed up with a full range of PR, direct marketing and online activities. Tourism Malaysia was able to do all this within its existing budget limits, even making savings along the way, while putting in place a programme of activities that led directly to significantly more visitors from the target countries and an increased share of wallet.

The huge task of implementing our 300 recommendations involved every part of the Tourism Malaysia organisation, working alongside a large team of more than 60 Fusionbrand staff and subcontractors.

There were several quick wins that we were able to secure almost immediately, such as the creation of a corporate identity brand manual that led to a new consistency of content, design and presentation and major savings in collateral production and distribution costs. This took less than three months. Tourism Malaysia's ramshackle collection of websites were consolidated and streamlined and regional PR agencies were appointed, each working to a clear and consistent brief. Tracking and measurement were given the highest priority and activities that were identified as unproductive and impossible to measure were scrapped, freeing up cash and other resources for use on more important aspects of the brand plan.

Other elements of the plan, such as the programme of staff workshops and training sessions, took longer to pay off. As the momentum built up, the 12 country-specific brand plans we had developed were rolled out, covering every aspect of brand building, from social media, advertising and PR activity to promotional and cultural events, local trade shows and new publications targeting specific customer segments.

In the year that followed, the strategy Fusionbrand had developed for Tourism Malaysia was implemented at home and abroad, leading to a co-ordinated, coherent set of activities that produced an impressive rise in visitor numbers and laid the foundations for future growth. The investment in detailed, meticulous customer research and careful *auditing of brand and communication effectiveness was fully vindicated by the results that were achieved.*

From my point of view, the hard work and effort we had predicted before we won the contract was all worth while. As I had anticipated, it was the application of a disciplined, research-based and data-driven methodology that underpinned our success, rather than any dazzling, off-the-wall creative brilliance.

But this careful, research-based process was not about finding quick fixes. It was about working towards solutions, rather than backing hunches and jumping to conclusions, and providing a factual, realistic foundation for the agency's future activities – not just for one year, but for several years ahead.

In the end, we worked with Tourism Malaysia for four years, under three different tourism ministers, from the initial research and planning stages right through to the detailed work of putting the strategy into practice. By the time the overarching brand plan had been successfully implemented, Tourism Malaysia had been transformed into an organisation that knew exactly where it wanted to go and had the tools, techniques and ideas to meet and exceed all its targets, from steadily increasing visitor numbers to consistently high customer satisfaction levels. As a demonstration of the Fusionbrand approach to profitable brand building, there could hardly be a better case study.

'Many organisations I work with in Malaysia and SE Asia have been able to save as much as 50% of the money they used to spend on advertising.

They've done it by focusing on the end goal – building the brand – rather than the seductive, distracting, time-consuming and ferociously expensive interim goal of creating mass media ad campaigns'

CHAPTER 25

The Goal Is the Brand, and the Brand Is the Goal

Why brand consultants mean business

The main aim of this book is to draw your attention to the fact that a lot of the money you are spending on trying to build your brand is almost certainly wasted.

That may sound harsh, and it may sound like bad news.

But, of course, it's not.

You can change it.

Because the good news is that you don't have to keep pouring money down the drain of mass media advertising. The world has changed. You have real options now that didn't exist even ten years ago.

Companies vary, and your circumstances may be special, but I have found that many of the organisations I work with in Malaysia and the other countries of Southeast Asia have been able to save as much as 50% of the money they used to spend on advertising.

They've done it simply by focusing on the end goal – building the brand – rather than the seductive, distracting, time-consuming and ferociously expensive interim goal of creating mass media advertising campaigns.

For the advertising agencies, naturally, big campaigns are

an end in themselves. That's what they get paid for. For their clients, it's different. If you are running a business and trying to build a brand that will grow and weather any storms or crises for years to come, the brand itself must be the goal.

Advertising should only ever have been one element in the way you got there. Instead, for the best part of a century, it managed to hypnotise the world into thinking it was the one way – the Only Way – to launch a product, build awareness, reach target markets, satisfy customers' practical and emotional needs, make sales and win market share, build a brand personality, create love and loyalty and guarantee repeat business.

But advertising is not just *not* the Only Way. It's not even a very good way of doing half these things. And whether it's working or not, it's always costing.

In the Eighties and early Nineties, I was as guilty as anyone else of not seeing the wood for the trees. Advertising seemed like the only real tool we had to work with, so we worked with it. As Abraham Maslow said, more than half a century ago: 'To the man with a hammer, every problem looks like a nail.' I hammered away at one ad campaign after another, trying to do what I could with the tools we had available at that time.

What has changed – apart from huge demographic, economic and business changes around the world, of course – is the arrival of the internet.

Standing back and looking at it now, it's obvious that as soon as we had the internet we'd have Google and YouTube, Amazon and eBay, smartphones and tablets, online shopping and social media. But standing back even further, what is the essence of all that change? Interactivity – 'two-wayness' – is the fundamental key that let the internet unlock a new world of potential change.

And in this interactive, two-way world, overpriced one-way corporate advertising campaigns that talk down to consumers and customers are not the key to building your brand.

I admit I didn't see all this coming. Tim Berners-Lee completely failed to tip me off about that World Wide Web he was inventing. So I got a lot of things wrong before I started to tune in and get them right. But I have always liked to learn from the wisdom of great men – scientists, generals, statesmen and philosophers – and from the spectacular cock-ups most of them have made on the way to achieving glory.

As one of the greatest of them all, Groucho Marx (or was it actually Sam Levenson, or Eleanor Roosevelt?) said, 'Learn from the mistakes of others. You can't live long enough to make them all yourself.'

The fact is, most of the branding mistakes being made today were also made yesterday. Yet few companies are learning from them.

That creates real opportunities, right now, for those who are ready to learn and prepared to do things differently. But if you want to move away from the expensive slavery imposed on business by the glitz and myths of the advertising industry, don't go to an advertising agency for advice. It won't be impartial.

It's time to contact a brand consultant.

The 21st century has already seen monumental changes in the consumer landscape. Consumers are exposed to more brands in just about every sector than ever before. And the way we source data about those brands, the way we interact with them, how we absorb information about them and what we want and expect from those brands has changed 180 degrees.

Before, we listened to what the brands told us. We gave a cursory nod to what we could learn of other consumers' opinions and experiences, but, on the whole, we believed what the advertisers wanted us to believe. Today, the boot's on the other foot. Other consumers – delighted customers or furiously disappointed complainers – are the people who define what a brand means. It's not the brand owner's call any more. At the same time, the way we shop and make purchasing decisions related to the brands we buy has changed beyond recognition.

In the boom days of marketing, from the 1950s through to the 1990s, the strategic goal – as far as there was one – was all about reaching the biggest, broadest audience, in the hope that the message would stick with enough of them. Advertising agencies defined and controlled a brand's message, in a way that was often quite loosely based on the needs of the company, and effectively took most of the main decisions about which media were to be used for each campaign and which channels it was broadcast on.

Consumers, facing a limited range of products and with little access to objective information, based many of their choices on what they were told in the adverts. Sometimes they were convinced that a product or service was sufficient for their needs. Often it wasn't, but they persuaded themselves they should make do with it anyway because there was no obvious alternative.

The be-all and end-all of marketing was to be the Brand Leader. And brand leadership was largely self-perpetuating. If this docile and uninformed public knew your name, consumers would buy, over and over again. 'Why risk your money on a product you've never heard of?' people said.

The logic for brand owners was clear cut. Spend. Spend on advertising, and spend as big as you can. Get the name out there, keep it out there and keep on spending. In the words of British singer-songwriter Elvis Costello, 'Pump it up.'

But the world really has changed, even if many of the big advertisers haven't noticed yet. The major global brands – and 80% of them are owned by just nine or ten vast multinationals – are still hurling many billions of dollars a year into their advertising campaigns. According to statista.com, global spending on advertising will reach US$537bn in 2015. Yet even Samsung, with its US$14bn marketing budget, is seeing diminishing returns on this gigantic spend, leading to its first annual loss in three years.

The worm has turned. It's a different world. Those days are over.

Today's better educated consumers have more choice than ever before and, thanks to the internet and social media, vastly more access to the experiences, opinions and knowledge of existing users. The belief that they will continue to be swayed by corporate messages shoved down their throats via channels they aren't interacting with is laughable.

Brand owners must understand that from now on, where, when and how they choose to spend their resources is critical to their long term success.

Consumers don't buy their messages any more. They won't take them at face value. They know they've been treated like fools, and they don't like it. They've heard too many horror stories about well-known and respected companies lying and cheating their way into the customer's wallet. They know that familiar names and an aura of respectability mean nothing, if only because of the VW emissions scandal and the behaviour of the big banks that have been caught out over and over again, fiddling exchange rates, mis-selling payment protection insurance and conniving in tax frauds. Trust can no longer be bought. It has to be earned.

Today, the vast majority of consumers expect quality, so long a key differentiator for many brands, to be a given.

They want banks to have a human face, petrol companies to have a community side, car manufacturers to stop lying about emissions and consumption figures and politicians to tell the truth and understand their needs.

They want brands to be what they say they are. And they

learn about these brands and whether they deliver what they promise not from advertising but from social networks, online communities and comparison websites – from the reports of others, as well as their own personal experiences.

This is where they look when seeking information on products and services. And this is probably just as well, because as brands frantically try to reach out to consumers, they are increasingly losing control of how and where their messages are communicated. Digital adverts for airlines pop up on news websites right alongside stories about aviation disasters. Banner ads for cars appear on auto sites that talk about the worst car crashes of all time and luxury chocolates are sold alongside tragic tales of famine in Africa. When the people and the algorithms that are running these campaigns aren't smart enough to stop these ghastly juxtapositions occurring, real harm is done – not to the media companies, of course, but to the brands involved. All these desperate attempts to sell product in the traditional way do nothing more than shut out consumers.

So does this mean the end of the line for advertising agencies and advertising? In the short term, probably not, because there is still a need for agencies to create good tactical work, and sometimes even to establish the very first contact with the potential customer. But the process has changed and the advertising agency can no longer be given responsibility for building your brand.

In the past, branding and advertising used to be elements of marketing.

Today, marketing and advertising are elements of branding, and it's the brand consultant you should look to if you want to build a brand.

If you haven't worked with a specialist brand consultant before, you may be wondering what the essential differences are. After all, many advertising agencies are scrambling to reposition and relabel themselves and pass themselves off as brand consultants. But there are some fundamental differences that no amount of window-dressing can hide.

Here is a brief outline that highlights eight of the main practical differences between an advertising agency and a brand consultancy. This should give you enough knowledge to make an informed decision about who you should work with as you start to develop and build your brand.

Brand consultancy vs advertising agency: the facts

1) Advertising is tactical; branding is strategic. The most strategic action you will usually get from an advertising agency will be the brief, the planning document that spells out the proposition the advertising must communicate and defines the market segments it should address. But then what? And what about internally? How will you get your personnel on brand? Is the advertising supposed to convince them as well? How is a glossy television or poster campaign supposed to communicate to your delivery driver and sales assistant the vital roles they each need to play in making sure your company lives up to its promises?

A brand consultant will look at the whole picture. Instead of jumping to the conclusion that every problem can be solved by throwing more money into conventional advertising campaigns, the brand consultant starts by carrying out a brand audit, a brand healthcheck. This is a detailed, rigorous research project that looks at your organisation, people, products and processes, as well as external factors like your markets and opportunities, where your potential customers spend their time online and who the influencers are in your industry. It gathers together a wide range of objective data and a host of different subjective views – from your customers, suppliers and distributors, from media pundits and opinion formers and from your own staff.

Like the advertising agency's brief, it highlights your strengths and the benefits that will make people want to buy from you. But it sets these alongside a realistic, clear-eyed view of what is going to be needed for your company to deliver, consistently and reliably, in ways that will delight your customers and make them enthusiastic supporters of your brand. This holistic view is quite different from the advertising agency's approach, and it lays the foundation for all the work that is to follow.

Once this 360° brand audit is completed, a brand consultant will use the information it has uncovered to develop a brand strategy and a brand plan or brand blueprint that will drive the brand strategy, both internally and externally. This will address dozens of key elements that affect the brand, from the copy that is used in recruitment advertising to the technology that supports your customer-facing departments, from the ability of your staff to represent the brand and deliver on your promises to the retention strategies you can use to keep customers coming back for more.

The brand consultant will work with you to determine the best resources to use to get the whole organisation on brand and functioning efficiently, and then go on to help you get the details right and put it all into practice, often over a period of two or three years. Try getting an ad agency to hang in there and do the heavy lifting with you once the excitement of the big campaign is over.

2) Advertising agencies do advertising. That's what they are good at – and some of them are very good indeed (though experience teaches that when the agency people impress you with a pitch, you should always check with them that the

creative work they're showing you was done by designers who still work for the agency). Advertising uses creativity and a slick message, backed up by a big media spend, to get the customer's attention. It does it via campaigns pushed out across many different platforms, such as TV, radio, billboards and the internet. More is better. And bigger is always better, too, it seems. The fact that the agency gets a commission for placing your ads with each of these channels shouldn't come into it, but you'd be naïve to think it doesn't.

Once you have settled on a creative campaign – probably after months of to-ing and fro-ing with the agency team – you launch it and keep your fingers crossed that your budget allows you to keep going long enough to break through the clutter. The problem is that this model is fatally flawed. It doesn't take into account the different value needs of your different customers and the level of their relationship with you. It's a bit like an aircraft manufacturer designing a single plane and trying to sell it to every airline around the world. If it's a small plane and the airline is looking for something to use on high-volume long haul routes, it's going to be a tough sale, no matter how good the aircraft might be.

If the first campaign doesn't work, or a crisis occurs, you either ask the agency to come up with another creative idea or get rid of the agency, hire another one and start the whole process again. The new agency will come up with a different angle and a different campaign, and try to convince you that this is the way forward, if only you are prepared to give it the budget it needs.

This model is flawed for several reasons, the most obvious being the fact that it requires you to have very deep pockets and a lot of time. Unless you create a campaign that resonates with consumers in all markets at the first attempt and can then afford to advertise heavily and consistently for long periods of time, this approach is simply going to waste valuable resources.

Building a brand requires you to know your limitations and your weaknesses, especially in relation to the brand experience. You must understand those weaknesses and address them, while taking into account what you are doing right and discovering how to make the most of that.

The problem with advertising agencies is that they consistently put the cart before the horse. Before you even attempt to communicate with anyone, you must identify and fix any weaknesses in the processes and systems required to deliver great products and services to your customers. As I've said so many times throughout this book, you must understand your customers' desire for economic, experiential and emotional (and, increasingly, social) value and identify how you can deliver that value on their terms, so they are happy to come back again and again. The answer, in some industries, may involve advertising, as one part of the solution. But a comprehensive approach to building the brand will also look at improving R&D, sales, production, supply chains, operations, customer relationships and retention strategies. These operational areas are critical to the success of the brand, and they are areas few advertising agencies know or understand.

3) Branding is a strategic institutional initiative, not a marketing project. Leaving it in the hands of the marketing department is a dereliction of duty. Any properly thought-out brand development programme must be driven from the top, and an experienced brand consultant will always insist on having C-level involvement right from the start, so that your brand strategy is where it should be, in the hands of executive management.

Contrast this with the advertising agency approach, where your strategy will usually be in the hands of a creative director and an account team with very little experience of the nitty-gritty realities of day-to-day business. However hard these bright young people try to put themselves in your place and understand what your company is trying to do, they are unlikely to be equipped for the task. They will default to doing what they do best, and hope that they can paper over their lack of understanding by distracting your attention with some sparkling new creative theme.

When an advertising agency wins your business, it will often go on a recruiting drive. If it's short of staff with the right expertise and credibility, it may try to hire new faces with experience in your industry.

Unfortunately, when the right talent isn't available, perhaps because these people are working for competitor agencies that have also won major accounts, you may end up with a lower level creative team working on your campaign. If this happens, you may never know, as the agency will be at pains to hide it from you. But you can take it from me that it happens all the time. And it does nothing at all to boost your chances of success.

4) Advertising agencies measure success in ways that don't put their clients' interests first. They are seen as successful if they win lots of awards for creativity. But your aim is not to have pretty or witty advertising – it's to build a strong, engaging and durable brand. Creative awards may help the agency, but they won't help you. There are few prizes (the UK Institute of Practitioners in Advertising's annual Effectiveness Awards are an honourable exception) that are handed out on the basis of an advertising campaign's success in increasing sales or profitability.

Luckily, there aren't many awards for brand consultants. This is a good thing, because it cuts out a lot of potentially distracting hype and allows them to focus on how best to develop and strengthen relationships with stakeholders and customers, which will always be the key to your brand's future.

5) Most advertising focuses on using a series of tactical campaigns to acquire new buyers. There's very little advertising aimed at retaining customers. The departments responsible for retention programmes are often bad at sharing information with other parts of the business, though it is obvious to anyone that elements like after-sales service and the handling of enquiries and complaints are vital and depend on good, specific information.

A good brand consultant will help you develop a strategy that covers both acquisition and retention and work with you to define what is needed to talk to both new and old customers, increase the brand's share of wallet and leverage positive relationships to create enthusiastic and credible customer advocates.

6) Traditional marketing activity is enormously wasteful, as much of the advertising that's put out falls on deaf ears – talking to irrelevant demographics, customers who cannot afford to buy or are not interested in the product or people who are simply not paying attention. A recent British study quoted in the *Harvard Business Review* said 72% of CEOs were tired of being asked for money from their marketing departments without any proper explanation of how increased spending would increase business. That's not just a British problem, and it may sound painfully familiar to you, too.

In the same survey, 77% of CEOs said they'd had enough of empty talk about 'brand equity' that couldn't be linked to any real equity. A properly thought-out brand programme will ensure budgets are spent on the right tactics for the right segments, with measures in place to allow business effectiveness to be monitored and quantified. It will include metrics to track promotions, sales, usage, intentions, purchase intent, influencers, sources of information, advertising and many other key business factors.

7) The advertising agency approach is based on a one-size-fits-all series of tactical advertising campaigns that use mass media and mass marketing techniques. Digital activities often tamely mirror traditional marketing, and fail to take into account the different ways consumers interact with digital channels.

A good brand programme will make full use of a range of specialist tools designed for the new technologies to collect and leverage specific data. This makes it possible to develop targeted communications across digital channels to engage prospects, while carrying on two-way conversations with existing customers.

8) Advertising agencies will often look at what the competition is doing and try to position an offering in relation to its competitors. This approach is flawed because successful organisations are nimble, almost by definition. By the time you have developed your position, the competition's strategy will have evolved and something different will be needed.

Brand consultants have seen this kind of awkward situation too often, and they won't want to let it occur again. A properly designed brand programme will be aware of what competitors are doing and use that knowledge to strengthen the firm's competitive advantage, but will never let competitors' activity dictate the brand's strategy.

'It may be different on Mars, but this is a fundamental fact of human nature here on Earth.

People don't like feeling they're being manipulated to boost an uncaring company's profits. If they decide for themselves that they like us and what we do, they are much more likely to recommend us to friends'

CHAPTER 26

Talking with Martians

Two intelligent beings from the red planet ask some of the key questions about the shift from advertising to a subtler, more durable approach to building and sustaining brands.

Why do companies need to get out of their bad habits? Why are after-sales service and customer retention so important in today's changing marketplace? What can social media do that advertising can't? And how can Southeast Asian firms punch above their weight by using their brains, instead of advertising brawn?

MARTIAN 1: What first convinced you that 'Stop advertising, start branding' was the right way to go?

Marcus Osborne: Well, there wasn't any one moment of revelation. It was more a question of seeing the evidence build up steadily over several years. First, there was the way Apple made the iPhone the best-known product in the world by focusing on service and disseminating positive product reviews to drive the product narrative.

The second realisation came when I discovered Samsung had spent US$14 billion on advertising in 2014, only to announce its first year-on-year loss in three years in early 2015. I noticed, too, that Microsoft had gone from 95% of the consumer market to 25%, despite spending US$9 billion on advertising. Meanwhile the market share of Malaysia's national car company, Proton, had crashed from 80% to less than 20%, despite massive advertising, and Volvo was wasting billions in its forlorn attempt to convince consumers that its dull, solid, reliable cars were actually exciting and charismatic dream machines.

I remember, too, learning that 80% of the world's consumer products were owned by 10 companies and that between them they were spending US$50 billion on advertising annually. Even if this model worked, I thought, how many Southeast Asian firms could afford the kind of budget that would let them compete head-on with that sort of firepower?

Another defining moment was when Malaysia Airlines Flight MH370 went missing in 2014 and I calculated that the airline had probably spent more than US$300 million on advertising in the years leading up to the tragedy. The fallout from that disaster virtually destroyed the airline, despite all that investment in advertising, because the carrier had nothing in the goodwill bank to help it survive. Another key moment was when I saw the expensive and wasteful launch campaign in Malaysia's *New Straits Times* for Wonda Coffee and thought to myself, 'Why on earth is this company trying to build its market share in such an old-fashioned, one-dimensional way?'

MARTIAN 2: What can social media do for us that advertising can't?

M.O: One big mistake Asian firms often make is to think that digital, including social, is just another channel – a new alternative to TV, radio and billboards. But that's really missing the point. If you learn to think differently and exploit its full potential, it can do things that no advertising campaign can ever achieve.

I saw a stunning example of how a good idea can catch on and develop a life and momentum of its own when we worked with a fitness centre in Singapore. The client's original idea was that we should work together to create a bunch of ads that could be placed on national news sites right after Chinese New Year.

The logic seemed right, if it was just a question of trying to deliver sales messages to potential customers at a time when they were likely to be thinking about getting fit again and working off the excesses of the holiday season. But we had a better idea up our sleeve – one with much more long-term potential.

The big problem with fitness clubs is customer churn – you can lose a quarter of your hard-won customers every year. So we suggested our client should focus, instead, on making the club more valuable to its existing customers, strengthening the sense of community among members and thus building greater customer loyalty. More specifically, we wanted to encourage members to interact with each other and share details of their workouts online, as happens on the Nike+ website. We set up web pages that allowed gym users to track their activity and compare their exercise times with those of others in the club, as well as with their own previous times.

We knew this would help club members motivate themselves to do better. What we didn't expect, even in our wildest dreams, was the way the project created its own social ecosystem, as hundreds of members took up the idea. Various fitness and nutrition-related brands were soon joining in with special offers and the original project quickly evolved into a whole range of gym and social activities based on the relationships that developed between members, many of whom had never spoken to each other before. Within a few weeks, one couple even started dating.

Our clients were delighted, of course, and their customer retention rates hit record levels, while word-of-mouth recommendations from enthusiastic participants brought in a steady flow of new customers. The catalyst for all this was the fitness centre's investment in the brand. It had created a positive buzz, boosted membership, attracted new business partners, provided extra value for existing customers – and even delivered love – all at a fraction of the cost of an advertising campaign.

MARTIAN 2: OK. That's impressive. But what about businesses where you don't have the opportunity to build that kind of social community. How has online shopping changed branding, for example?

M.O: Online shopping has changed the branding business on many different levels, including making it far easier to retain customers. The best e-commerce firms use slick data collection and communication technologies and clever, competitive pricing to keep their customers and induce them to spend more.

This means, in turn, that these customers have less to spend with their competitors. If these competitors are investing heavily in advertising, they will be wasting their time. Customers who have spent all their money and feel loyalty and goodwill towards their established online favourites aren't going to suddenly switch their allegiance to a new supplier because of an ad campaign.

MARTIAN 1: I noticed you mentioned earlier that your clients usually commission you to undertake brand audits for them. Why is that necessary? Why do you need to do a brand audit?

M.O: Because it is practically impossible to build a brand efficiently and cost effectively without doing a thorough brand audit first.

The brand audit provides the essential information you need to plan the right route for the brand journey. It provides the backbone for the development of the brand narrative.

A good brand audit gives you a realistic, unflinching snapshot of where your brand stands. It looks at every facet of the brand and its ability to communicate, engage and deliver value to customers. It makes sure everyone in the company is reflecting the brand values in every contact with the customers and that the brand is talking to the right people in the right way and at the right time. Without a rigorous audit and a clear understanding of what's good, what's acceptable and what needs more work, all your branding efforts will be nothing more than shooting in the dark.

MARTIAN 2: I understand that social media is great for getting through to the kids. But how effective is it in reaching the grown-up customers who hold the purse-strings and have the real purchasing power?

M.O: Our approach doesn't just rely on social media to build brands. 'Don't *do* social,' we always say. '*Be* social.'

In practice, it's all about taking the brand to the consumer and helping him or her to learn about it organically. These days, creating a positive social media presence isn't just about exploiting the power and potential of Facebook, Twitter and Snapchat or Pinterest. It's also about blogs, forums, product review sites and more. It's a serious mistake to think of social as just being for the young. Every age and every demographic is spending more time being social – and that's a trend that's not going to go away.

MARTIAN 1: What can Southeast Asian firms do to use their marketing budgets more effectively?

M.O: Asian brands must open up and see staff as an investment, not a cost. They must become more accessible and transparent and see customers as collaborators. They must understand that they need to engage their customers, collect data about them, be nice to them and do things for them that traditionally they wouldn't have done. They must build genuine two-way relationships with them, listening hard and understanding the long-term business value of customer engagement, retention and other tools.

Asian brand owners also need to understand that enthusiastic reviews on respected blogs and review sites (and the conversations that follow) are more valuable than any advertising campaign, no matter how creative. They are the key to successful brand building. They must learn to engage both blog owners and the people who respond with their comments and to share those reviews across the ecosystem to make the most of every positive mention.

This has become an urgent priority, and it's not something Asian firms can opt out of. The change can be a scary experience for many C-level executives in Asian companies, because it creates a more human, informal and transparent environment, shifts control of the brand's destiny away from the company and puts it in the hands of the customer, and makes it harder to hide inferior goods or low quality work.

MARTIAN 1: So to build brands, Southeast Asian firms must change?

M.O: Yes. They must. Change is inevitable. Chief executives in our region must look to build more inclusive, modern and human companies that consumers, staff and other stakeholders can buy into wholeheartedly. Southeast Asian firms must work to create an innovative, positive, customer-focused culture that encourages internal collaboration and empowers employees to take the initiatives that will make them more efficient and customer-centric. This process is essential if you are to build an enviable reputation for your brand and better relationships with existing customers, which can then be translated into better conversion rates, increased loyalty and a larger share of wallet.

MARTIAN 2: How important is after-sales service in building today's brands?

M.O: Customer service interactions have a vital role to play in successful brand building. Companies simply cannot afford to go missing when there are problems with their products.

My Up fitness-tracking wristband was a case in point. I stuck with it for nine months, even though it kept breaking, over and over again. I put up with this far longer than I normally would, because the manufacturer, Jawbone, didn't hide from me (as a lot of Southeast Asian firms will do) but genuinely engaged with me and tried to deal with my problem. The company's customer service response was fast and efficient and Jawbone happily replaced the product three times, despite the fact that it does not operate in Malaysia. I'm not normally all that patient with products that fail, but, like other consumers, I am always inclined to be more forgiving than usual when I can see the company I'm dealing with is going out of its way to be helpful and approachable.

This carefully nurtured relationship finally fell apart because the smart band broke for the fourth or fifth time and I became fed up with the whole process. Besides, I thought, any product that has such a high failure rate won't survive for long. I'm still in the market for another smart fitness and activity tracking band, but this time I won't buy anything until I've read plenty of consumer reviews and looked at the relevant comparison sites.

MARTIAN 2: But can you really rely on opinions you read in customer reviews? Why are social media and comparison and review sites so important?

M.O: Well, which do you trust more – information you have found that appears to come from an impartial source or information from advertisers and marketers that have targeted you as a likely customer?

The fact is, none of us is all that ready to trust someone who is setting out to persuade us to buy a particular product or service. We are much more likely to be influenced by a positive comment that comes from someone with no axe to grind.

It may be different on Mars, but this is a fundamental fact of human nature here on Earth. Advertising is overtly manipulative, and people don't like the feeling that they are being manipulated to boost an uncaring company's profits.

That's why we use content and relationships in social media and other online channels to allow consumers to build their own understanding of a brand. If they decide for themselves that they like us and what we do, they are much more likely to recommend us to friends and to post positive – and influential – comments online.

I came across one great example of how this process works in an interesting and provocative book called *Absolute Value*, by Itamar Simonson and Emanuel Rosen. The authors, a Stanford University professor and a software marketing expert, talk about a huge research study, a few years ago, that asked 10,000 people around the world if they would buy a sophisticated but expensive digital gadget that combined the functions of a mobile phone, an email terminal, an MP3 music player and a camera.

The researchers concluded that consumers were so content with their existing phones, cameras and digital music players that they simply wouldn't pay a premium for an all-in-one device.

When the product was launched, though, the early reviews were so positive and enthusiastic, and shared so widely and so quickly, that the iPhone became an overnight sensation. It is now the most famous phone – and perhaps brand – in the world, and the basis for Apple's recordbreaking business profits.

MARTIAN 1: But won't companies still need to advertise to reach consumers?

M.O: What's the point of reaching consumers if everyone else is reaching them, too? They may not hear your message, and they certainly won't be listening. Nobody in the advertising industry wants to believe it, but consumers work very hard to tune out almost all of the thousands of mass media advertising messages that bombard them every day.

And advertising is also painfully ineffective online. I was reading a report the other day that claimed only one person in a thousand who sees an online ad will click on it. What's worse, just 8% of internet users account for 85% of all clicks on banner ads.

Even low response rates like this may not be available for long. Free tools such as Adblock Plus (which already claims 300 million downloads) are becoming increasingly popular, which means many potential customers may not even see traditional online ad campaigns in the future. But there are other innovative tools, such as dynamic remarketing (you know, when you've viewed something online and then it follows you around the web for weeks – even, illogically and infuriatingly, *after* you have made a purchase), that have considerable potential. It is important to stay abreast of developments in advertising technologies, but, with a few specialised exceptions, advertising simply isn't the best way for today's firms to build their brands.

MARTIAN 2: OK, Marcus. What's the best example you can give us of how you've helped your customer boost profits?

M.O: We were working a couple of years ago with a Malaysian developer that had been using ad campaigns to sell properties but wasn't happy with the results. Fusionbrand was brought in to review the company's communications, to carry out a customer experience audit, to examine the way the sales force worked and to recommend the best way forward.

We soon saw the big opportunity our client had been missing. The new developments were much more upmarket than earlier projects. These luxury villas and apartments were beyond the budget of all but a small number of high net worth individuals and we were sure that advertising was a very inefficient way of trying to reach and persuade them. So we recommended that the developer should stop advertising – thus saving several million ringgit over a two-year period – and follow a strategy based on building deeper and more personal relationships with the select group of people who could afford to pay premium prices.

The results were spectacular. In eight months, 95% of the properties had been sold. The developer had been looking at a 24-month sales campaign, with all the staffing costs and overheads that entailed. Instead, the company was able to take its profit and move on, way ahead of schedule, to put its money to work again on the next luxury development.

It's important to remember, though, that financial profits are not always the objective. One government department we worked with called us in to carry out a digital communications audit and implement the long list of recommendations that emerged from the audit's findings. This organisation credited our ideas and advice with transforming its operations, though it measured its success in terms of social, reputational and even political gains, rather than cash profits.

MARTIAN 1: I meant to ask you before, why do you believe customer retention is so important in building a brand?

M.O: First, because it costs so much to acquire a customer, you'd be mad not to do whatever it takes, within reason, to hang on to that buyer. This is especially true in SE Asia, where acquiring customers is so often based on the short-term appeal of low prices. Without a robust, effective retention strategy, you will always be stuck in a price war with your competitors. The loser of that war goes out of business (and quite often the victor does as well – winning a price war is often a costly triumph).

After all, historically, 80% of all purchases are repeat purchases. Does it really make sense to spend a fortune going after the 20%, if you can avoid it?

Second, it's always easier and cheaper to sell to an existing customer, someone who has already bought from you. It should generally be more profitable to focus on getting these people to buy from you again, and even spend more with you, than to try to persuade people who haven't spent anything with you to take the plunge for the first time.

Third, and most important of all, your happy, loyal customers will share their experiences with others. If you can get engaged in the development of that narrative and nudge it in the direction you want, you may well find that recommendations from your existing customers take care of all your acquisition needs.

MARTIAN 1: Aren't companies scared of making this kind of major change? I've heard people say: 'My advertising may be inefficient, but I do know how to do it. And besides I get the agency to do all the heavy lifting and if they get it wrong I can find another agency. I'd be a complete beginner in areas like social media and I might get it badly wrong.' Isn't it generally better for them to play safe and stick to what they know?

M.O: No. Definitely not. To put it bluntly, you can't afford to ignore social media these days. Facebook is where 43% of B2B companies and 77% of B2C companies find customers. And it's not surprising. Some days, Facebook has one billion active users in the 24-hour period. How can you not be there?

The good news, though, is that it is relatively easy to learn to use social media.

You just need to take it slowly, understand what you are doing and why, and then make sure you integrate everything you do on social media with the other platforms and CRM tools in your armoury. It'll take you a few months to crank up the number of followers and engage them. But once you do, the stronger relationships and direct and instant connection with your followers will pay off in terms of shorter sales cycles, increased sales and higher profits.

MARTIAN 2: This stuff's OK for California, but what makes you so sure the new approach you're recommending can work in SE Asian companies?

M.O: We're not really advocating a new approach. We're advocating using your money more carefully, more effectively, more relevantly and with greater accountability – because, frankly, too much money has traditionally been wasted on pointless, unprofitable advertising.

This is actually more important for SE Asian companies than it is in California, because SE Asian companies often have to work harder than established US and European firms to create trust and credibility and build a customer base – even in their home markets. And nurturing trust and credibility is not something that can be done with advertising and other traditional tools.

Take TV advertising. It's hugely expensive and firms have to spend vast amounts of money to reach TV audience members who often aren't in the same room when the commercial airs or are busy on their mobile devices. Television and the other mass media just aren't getting through any more – if they ever did. In Indonesia, for example, passenger car sales have been stagnant for years, despite year by year increases in advertising budgets across the board.

MARTIAN 1: What is wrong with traditional marketing theories about positioning? Surely the same rules apply, even in this brave new world of yours?

M.O: Positioning was developed over 40 years ago, and quickly became a key element in every marketing strategy. But the world really has changed a lot since then. Consumers are busier and more cynical, and they're used to having more choice than ever before. What's more, how consumers get their information, where they go for it and who influences them have changed, too, beyond all recognition.

Companies no longer define brands, consumers do. And they define them based on the experiential, emotional and economic value those brands are able to deliver, rather than on any claims or imagery put together by the companies that own them.

MARTIAN 2: If organisations stop advertising and the brand-building strategy doesn't work for them, they could find they've lost most of their customer base in a few months. You're asking people to take a huge risk, aren't you?

M.O: Most brands don't even know whether advertising is really responsible for creating awareness of their brand with the customers that buy their product or service. So a key part of the new brand-building strategy will be to take money you might have wasted on advertising and use it to focus more on your relationship with your customers.

You'll get a better understanding of their requirements for value and then be able to deliver that value to them. As the relationship grows, you'll learn more about your brand and how to make it better, as well as what makes your customers happy. That's not a strategy that will lose you customers. It will lead to those customers spending more money with you, more often, and telling others about their experiences, becoming an unpaid extension to your sales force. The risk is not moving in this direction. The risk is standing still, while the world changes all around you.

MARTIAN 1: If everybody decides to 'stop advertising, start branding', customers are going to be flooded with social media messages. Smaller firms are just going to be lost in the clutter, aren't they? So what happens then?

M.O: It's not just a matter of learning to use social media. You have to know what you are trying to achieve and why and how to adopt the technologies that will help you collect data on customers and use that data to build rapport. It's my job to help companies make their brands better. I'm helping them use new media, techniques and tools to understand their customers better and engage with them more frequently and with more relevant content, as a route to deeper relationships, improved loyalty and increased profits. The great advantage of using social media to engage consumers is that you can quickly build very personal relationships – and they cut right through the clutter and clamour of mass media advertising messages.

The aim must be to understand your customers as individuals – who they are, how they live, how and through which channels they prefer to be engaged and what they care about and value. If you can do that, you will have their attention and they will hear your voice. Get that right and it just doesn't matter what other companies are doing.

MARTIAN 1: Right. I see. One final question, then. Can social media really generate the sales needed to grow a business?

M.O: Certainly it can. I'll give you an example. One of my staff asked me recently if he could buy the book I mentioned earlier, *Absolute Value*, by Itamar Simonson and Emanuel Rosen. When I asked him why he thought it would be useful, he replied, 'Because of the reader comments on Amazon.'

I looked, and I could see his point. Here was a book that stood at number 60,000 in the Amazon charts – not, in itself, high enough to be much of a recommendation. But there were 36 reader reviews and most of them were very enthusiastic about it, giving it an overall rating of 4.7 out of 5. That went some way towards convincing me. This book had obviously not been noticed by all that many people, but it was clear that many of those who had come across it had found it a worthwhile read.

'OK,' I said. 'Buy it on the company's account – and pass it on to me when you've finished with it.'

When I read it, *Absolute Value* turned out to be one of the most realistic and thought-provoking business books I had seen for years. So I went back to my junior colleague and asked him how he had found out about it.

'I was reading about it in an article in the *Atlantic Magazine* online,' he said, 'and it said it was a really original, important book.'

I was surprised.

'Why on earth were you looking through *Atlantic Magazine*?' I asked. 'That's not your usual reading matter.'

'Oh no,' he said. 'I read the article because it came up when I Googled "Digital ads don't work." I'd never heard of the magazine before.'

No need for an advertising campaign, then. This purchase had been made because of a Google search, a magazine article and a collection of positive customer reviews on Amazon.

No-one could possibly have planned or engineered this exact sequence of events, but it had led directly to a sale – and to a lot more recommendations from me, both in conversations with friends and contacts and, of course, now, in the pages of a widely-read book.

Acknowledgements

This book has been inspired by the people at the sharp end, the branding, marketing and communications professionals, civil servants and business leaders I meet every day of my working life. People like you who are looking to build a brand but don't have the resources to go head to head with the big players. Or people like you who are frustrated by the ineffectiveness of traditional marketing but don't have the bandwidth to search for inspiration or alternative ideas. I hope my advice and experience will help you grow your brand without wasting money on ineffective, inefficient and outdated advertising campaigns.

I want to thank Nick Wreden for being such an incredible source of ideas and quotes, and Ian Shircore for professionalism way beyond the call of duty. Others who have been an inspiration for me include Michael Osborne, Harry and Claire Harrison, Robin, Amanda, Edward and Emily Gainsford, Gordon and Manuela James, Robert and Erika Remnant, Simon Eldon Edington, Ron Mathison and the many military men and women of my younger days.

Finally, I thank the four most important people in my life – Rafidah, Aisha, Aila and Adam – who put up with me through the extraordinary process of writing a book, contributed ideas, always encouraged me and never once suggested I do something proper with my life.

Index

Index

Index